D0651149

Sweetness & Lightning volume 1 is a work of fiction. Names, characters, places, and incidents are the products of the author's imagination or are used fictitiously. Any resemblance to actual events, locales, or persons, living or dead, is entirely coincidental.

A Kodansha Comics Trade Paperback Original.

Sweetness & Lightning volume 1 copyright © 2013 Gido Amagakure
English translation copyright © 2016 Gido Amagakure

All rights reserved.

Published in the United States by Kodansha Comics,
an imprint of Kodansha USA Publishing, LLC, New York.

Publication rights for this English edition arranged through Kodansha Ltd., Tokyo.

First published in Japan in 2013 by Kodansha Ltd., Tokyo, as *Ama-ama to Inadzuma* volume 1.

ISBN 978-1-63236-456-2

Printed in the United States of America.

www.kodanshacomics.com

9 8 7 6 5 4 3 2 1

Translation: Adam Lensenmayer
Lettering: Lys Blakeslee
Editing: Ajani Oloye
Kodansha Comics Edition Cover Design: Phil Balsman

KODANSHA COMICS
Yamada-kun and the Seven Witches
"A very funny manga with a lot of heart and character."
—Adventures in Poor Taste
SWAPPED WITH A KISS?!
Class troublemaker Ryu Yamada is already having a bad day when he stumbles down a staircase along with star student Urara Shiraishi. When he wakes up, he realizes they have switched bodies—and that Ryu has the power to trade places with anyone just by kissing them! Ryu and Urara take full advantage of the situation to improve their lives, but with such an oddly amazing power, just how long will they be able to keep their secret under wraps?
Available now in print and digitally!
© Miki Yoshikawa/Kodansha Ltd. All rights reserved.

Maria
THE VIRGIN WITCH
"Maria's brand of righteous justice, passion and plain talking make for one of the freshest manga series of 2015. I dare any other book to top it."
—UK Anime Network
PURITY AND POWER
As a war to determine the rightful ruler of medieval France ravages the land, the witch Maria decides she will not stand idly by as men kill each other in the name of God and glory. Using her powerful magic, she summons various beasts and demons —even going as far as using a succubus to seduce soldiers into submission under the veil of night— all to stop the needless slaughter. However, after the Archangel Michael puts an end to her meddling, he curses her to lose her powers if she ever gives up her virginity. Will she forgo the forbidden fruit of adulthood in order to bring an end to the merciless machine of war?
Available now in print and digitally!
KODANSHA COMICS
©Mayasuki Ishikawa /Kodansha, Ltd. All rights reserved.

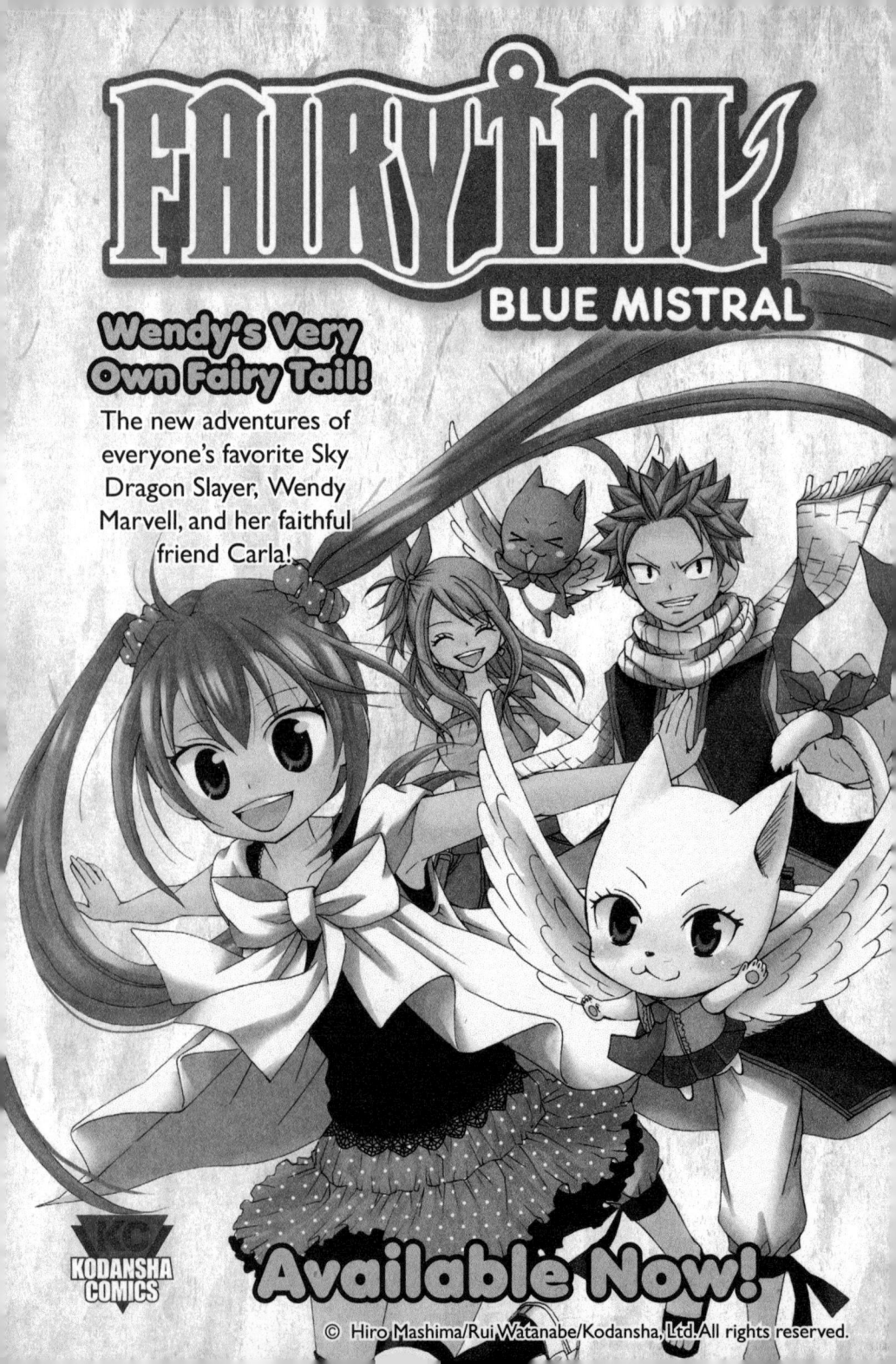
FAIRY TAIL
BLUE MISTRAL
Wendy's Very Own Fairy Tail!
The new adventures of everyone's favorite Sky Dragon Slayer, Wendy Marvell, and her faithful friend Carla!
KC
KODANSHA COMICS
Available Now!
© Hiro Mashima/Rui Watanabe/Kodansha, Ltd. All rights reserved.

KODANSHA COMICS
THE HEROIC LEGEND OF
ARSLAN
READ THE NEW SERIES FROM THE CREATOR OF FULLMETAL ALCHEMIST, HIROMU ARAKAWA! NOW A HIT TV SERIES!
"Arakawa proves to be more than up to the task of adapting Tanaka's fantasy novels and fans of historical or epic fantasy will be quite pleased with the resulting book."
-Anime News Network
ECBATANA IS BURNING!
Arslan is the young and curious prince of Pars who, despite his best efforts doesn't seem to have what it takes to be a proper king like his father. At the age of 14, Arslan goes to his first battle and loses everything as the blood-soaked mist of war gives way to scorching flames, bringing him to face the demise of his once glorious kingdom. However, it is Arslan's destiny to be a ruler, and despite the trials that face him, he must now embark on a journey to reclaim his fallen kingdom.
Available now in print and digitally!
© Hiromu Arakawa/Yoshiki Tanaka/Kodansha Ltd. All rights reserved.

a Silent Voice
KODANSHA COMICS
"The word heartwarming was made for manga like this." –Manga Bookshelf
"A harsh and biting social commentary... delivers in its depth of character and emotional strength." -Comics Bulletin
"A very powerful story about being different and the consequences of childhood bullying... Read it." –Anime News Network
Shoya is a bully. When Shoko, a girl who can't hear, enters his elementary school class, she becomes their favorite target, and Shoya and his friends goad each other into devising new tortures for her. But the children's cruelty goes too far. Shoko is forced to leave the school, and Shoya ends up shouldering all the blame. Six years later, the two meet again. Can Shoya make up for his past mistakes, or is it too late?
Available now in print and digitally!
© Yoshitoki Oima/Kodansha Ltd. All rights reserved.

Mei Tachibana has no friends — and says she doesn't need them!

But everything changes when she accidentally roundhouse kicks the most popular boy in school! However, Yamato Kurosawa isn't angry in the slightest—in fact, he thinks his ordinary life could use an unusual girl like Mei. But winning Mei's trust will be a tough task. How long will she refuse to say, "I love you"?

© Kanae Hazuki / Kodansha Ltd. All rights reserved.

NO.6
A PERFECT LIFE IN A PERFECT CITY
For Shion, an elite student in the technologically sophisticated city No. 6, life is carefully choreographed. One fateful day, he takes a misstep, sheltering a fugitive his age from a typhoon. Helping this boy throws Shion's life down a path to discovering the appalling secrets behind the "perfection" of No. 6.
KC
KODANSHA COMICS
© Atsuko Asano and Hinoki Kino/Kodansha Ltd. All rights reserved.

PRAISE FOR THE ANIME!
"This series never fails to put a smile on my face."
-Dramatic Reviews
"A very funny look at what happens when two strange and strangely well-suited people try to navigate the thorny path to true love together."
-Anime News Network
My Little Monster
OPPOSITES ATTRACT...MAYBE?
Haru Yoshida is feared as an unstable and violent "monster." Mizutani Shizuku is a grade-obsessed student with no friends. Fate brings these two together to form the most unlikely pair. Haru firmly believes he's in love with Mizutani and she firmly believes he's insane.
© Robico / Kodansha Ltd. All rights reserved.
KC
KODANSHA COMICS

A gratin filled with veggies.

Will it work?

Will Tsumugi smile...

...and say it's delicious?

甘々と稲妻 Sweetness & Lightning 2

On Sale September 2016!

sweetness & lightning

1

Gido Amagakure

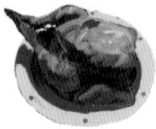

c o n t e n t s

Chapter 1
Uniforms and Donabe Rice
3

Chapter 2
Pork Miso Soup and Restaurant Lights
45

Chapter 3
Tsumugi and the Long-Awaited Salisbury Steak
79

Chapter 4
Golden Week and Packed Lunches
113

Chapter 5
Daddy's Restaurant: "You Got a Cold" Special
147

Chapter 1 Uniforms and Donabe Rice
BEEP
BEEP BEEP BEEP...
MMM...
SFFF...
MORNING, DADDY!
JERK
ぎゅっ
NGH.
S'MORNING!
すちゃ
CRINKLE
HEY!
TSUMUGI! YOU'RE STEPPING ON THE HAND-OUTS!
CLK
CRINKLE
HUH?
DON'T MOVE...
CURCLE CURCLE CURCLE

Chapter 1 Uniforms and Donabe Rice

OKAY!
SMACK
ばち
ばちっ
SMACK
YES, SIR!
WATCH IT WHILE YOU EAT BREAK-FAST.
SURE, SURE.
DADDY, CAN I WATCH MAGI-GAL?
I CAN'T FIND MY PINK MAGI-GAL OUT-FIT!
DADDY!
HOLD ON A SECOND.
I GOTTA BUY CHERRY TOMATOES...
PLUCK
さっ
PLUCK
GRAB
LOOKS LIKE YOUR REMARK WAS OFF THE MARK!
TRA LA LA
チャラ
DING
PACKAGES: FROZEN EDAMAME, FRIED CHICKEN
LEFT: JELLY

OKAY!
SUN-DAY'S GOING TO BE LAUNDRY DAY.
YELLOW MAGI-GAL IS STRONG TOO, RIGHT?!
OH NO! OUR NATION IS DOOMED!
WE DO HAVE YOUR YELLOW MAGI-GAL T-SHIRT, THOUGH.
It's not done yet...
AWW...
GOODBYE!
SLAM
ばたん!
ばたた
RUSH
DADDY, I'M STUCK!
UNDO THE BUT-TONS BEFORE YOU PUT IT ON.
ばたた
RUSH
EEEE!
HUCH A CU' GAHL.
VEH GOO
SO SHE'LL BE STAYING LATE TODAY, THEN.
THE SITTER WILL BE HERE TO PICK HER UP AT 4.
Bye byeee!
Good morning!
Good mooorning!
Good morning!

SLAM.
INU! ZUKA! SENSEI!
Erk.
RATTLE
GOOD MORNING.
MATH PREP ROO
GOOD MORNING.
SO ARE YOU COMING TO THE WELCOME-SLASH-GOODBYE PARTY?
YOU CAN BRING THE KID...
OH...
SORRY. I THINK I'M GOING TO SKIP IT AFTER ALL.

LOOK HOW THIN HE'S GETTING, THOUGH!
SCRAWNY
I THINK WE NEED TO FILL THAT BELLY OF HIS.
Huh... THAT'S A SHAME.
HE KIND OF HAS TO.
HIS DAUGHTER'S STILL LITTLE, YOU KNOW?
And it's at a bar...
MOMOYA-SENSEI, THAT'S REALLY NONE OF YOUR BUSINESS.
DON'T WORRY ABOUT ME.
I'VE NEVER BEEN A BIG EATER.
FLIP
I'VE ALSO TRIED COOKING ONCE, BUT...
...IT CAUSED MY DAUGHTER TO MAKE A FACE I'D NEVER SEEN BEFORE.
BWA-HA!
That's sooo cute!
Well, LATELY, EVEN THE CONVENIENCE STORE BOXED LUNCHES HAVE THE RIGHT AMOUNT OF CALORIES AND NUTRITION.
YEAH. IT'S A BIG HELP.

Okay!
Anyway, first period's starting.
GIVE HIM A BREAK...
HE REJECTED US AGAIN!
YAWN
IT'S ONLY BEEN SIX MONTHS SINCE HIS WIFE PASSED AWAY.
FLOWER-VIEWING?
I'LL GO!
...

ゴーン
RUMBLE
ゴーン
RUMBLE
VRRRR
カリ
Yay!
ME!
IF YOU CAN HELP, RAISE YOUR HAND.
SO CAN YOU HELP ME CLEAN UP UNTIL BOTH THE LITTLE HAND AND THE BIG HAND POINT STRAIGHT UP?
GOOD, GOOD.
PHEW...
DADDY, STUFF MR. GALI GALI IN YOUR SHIRT, OKAY?
CINCH
GOT IT.

OH?
WOBBLE
YOU OKAY?
HERE.
HUP!
MAYBE THIS WAS A BAD IDEA...
...
ざわざわ
MUR MUR
MUR MUR
Ha ha ha ha
Yeah!
IT'S PRETTY CROWDED...
Ha ha ha
OH?
THERE ARE A LOT OF PEOPLE HERE!
DON'T LOOK AT THE PEOPLE. LOOK AT THE FLOWERS.

GULP

Hey!
TSUMUGI, YOU STARTLED HER!
Oh...
NO, I'M FINE.
HUH?
ARE YOU OKAY?
FLIP
くるっ
スタッ
TAP
I'M CRYING BECAUSE THIS FOOD IS DELICIOUS.
IT MEANS SHE DIDN'T COME.
YUP!
WHEN DID SHE LEARN THAT?
DO YOU KNOW WHAT THAT MEANS?
MY MOM PROMISED TO MEET ME, BUT SHE FLAKED...
I ATE IT ALL, THOUGH!
THIS WASN'T JUST FOR ME. IT WAS ORIGINALLY MEANT FOR TWO PEOPLE.
CLACK
I SEE.
HUH?
UM, I MEAN...
I'M NOT CRYING BECAUSE I'M LONELY.

AND SO...
...I GOT MAD.
BUT THE FOOD WAS GOOD, EVEN IF I WAS ALONE.
SO I STARTED THINKING ABOUT HOW SHE MADE IT.
I KNOW SHE'S BUSY...
AS I ATE, I JUST KEPT REMEMBERING THINGS...
...AND THEN...
...I STARTED CRYING, FOR SOME REASON.
I SEE.
...SORRY, IT'S ALL GONE.
YOU ATE IT ALL BY YOURSELF?
Uh...
YES, I ATE IT ALL BY MYSELF!
WAS IT THAT GOOD?
DROOL
ダー

CARD: MEGUMI RESTAURANT

SIGN: DRAGON HOT BENTO (BOXED LUNCH)

NOPE!
HEH HEH...
ぎゅっ
SQUEEZE
...
YOU DON'T WANT ONE? WOULD YOU RATHER EAT OUT?
BOXED LUNCHES AGAIN?
The light of hooope!
Magical!
Magi-Gal!
HUP!
もぞ
RUSTLE
SHOVE
Nah...
I'LL TALK TO MOM...
I WANT TO DO AS MUCH AS I CAN ON MY OWN.
I THINK WE NEED TO START EATING MEALS AT HOME.

HM?
HMM...
...ABOUT THIS GOOD?
...
HOW WAS YOUR DINNER?
I ATE IT!
SHOVE SHOVE
じじ...
HOW ABOUT A "THANK YOU"?
THANKS FOR THE FOOD!
うちゅ
SMOOCH
OH!
I HAVE NO IDEA HOW GOOD THAT IS...
FEEL BETTER?
Awww...
KISS KISS!
ZOOM!
GYAH!
Ha ha ha!
THANKS! GOTCHA BACK!

KA-SHH
カシュ
THE WIND WAS STRONG TODAY.
WE WERE LUCKY THERE WERE STILL SOME CHERRY BLOSSOMS LEFT.
CLUNK
コト

...

KA-CHAK
ガチャ!
I'M BACK!
SORRY! THE SITTER ALREADY LEFT, RIGHT?

TSU-MU...
TSU-MUGI?
WOW!
THAT LOOKS SOOO GOOD!
YES! IF YOU USE THE "PERFECT PRO" PRESSURE COOKER, COOKING CAN BE THIS QUICK AND EASY!
LOOK AT HOW TENDER THIS MEAT IS!

CRASH
SEND A LETTER TO MOMMY AND TELL HER TO MAKE THIS!
RUMBLE
GURGLE
DAD-DY.
LET'S EAT SOME-THING YUMMY TODAY, OKAY?
REALLY ?!
TO GET FOOD.
WHERE ARE WE GOING ?
Huff
DASH
DASH
Huff
DASH

BEEP
Hello?
HELLO! THIS IS INU-ZUKA.
YOU GAVE ME YOUR BUSINESS CARD THE OTHER DAY.
OH...
I'M SORRY, WE'RE CLOSED TODAY.
PLEASE! WE'RE ALREADY ON OUR WAY!
NO, STILL, WE... I MEAN...
PLEASE!

I WANT TO GIVE MY DAUGHTER SOMETHING GOOD TO EAT!

IS THIS IT?
OH!
WHAT TIME IS IT?
...
OKAY.
IF THIS IS ABOUT MAGI-GAL, I RECORD-ED IT.
Magi Magic, the light of...
YOU SING TOO, DADDY!
SURE THING.
Magi

THE
LIGHT
OF
HOPE...
CLATTER
カラ…

HUH?
...

UM...
YOU'RE THE GIRL FROM BEFORE?
She's prettier than I remember...
YES, THAT'S RIGHT.
BOW
ペコ
NICE TO SEE YOU AGAIN.
SHE'S OUT HELPING SOMEONE WHO'S DONE A LOT FOR US...
もごっ
MUMBLE
もごっ
MUMBLE
MY MOM IS...WELL...
I...
I DON'T REALLY EAT A LOT...
...AND I DON'T KNOW WHAT'S POPULAR.
I SEE...
GLOOM
ズーン

IS THERE ANYPLACE GOOD AROUND HERE?
WE'RE THE BEST AROUND HERE!
SURE, MY MOTHER ISN'T HERE...
...BUT YOU CAN'T ASK ME TO GIVE YOU THE NAME OF ONE OF OUR RIVALS!
No...
...that's not...
...what I meant...
I...
I CAN AT LEAST...
DONABE
...COOK SOME RICE, YOU KNOW!
Uh...
UM...
PLEASE TAKE A SEAT!
GO AHEAD!
A NABE POT!
IS RICE FROM A POT GOOD?
It's a clay pot, 'kay?
IT'S SUPER-GOOD!

SHAKE
WHY IS SHE DOING THIS...?
SWISH
SWISH
SWISH
GLUG
GLUG
GLUG
SWISH
SHHH
SWISH
SWISH
SWISH
SWISH
SWISH
SWISH
SWISH
SWISH
SWISH
GLUG GLUG GLUG...

SWISH
ジャッ

Mm.
...
WHEW...

DADDY'S GONNA GO TO THE BATHROOM.
POOPIES?
No!

...

UM...
PARDON ME FOR A MOMENT.
Oh
SURE.

UGH, MOMMM!
?!
C'MON, HELP ME...
MUMBLE
MUMBLE
MUMBLE
?
WHAT'S A CUP? HOW MUCH IS IT? IF YOU HEAR THIS MESSAGE, PLEASE GIVE ME A CALL!
WHY DON'T DONABE HAVE THE MARKS ON THE INSIDE FOR COOKING RICE? I TRIED TO BE COOL AND SAID I COULD MAKE IT!
SORRY TO KEEP YOU WAITING.
キリッ
DIGNIFIED
...ARE YOU OKAY?
WHY WOULD I NOT BE?
SNEAK
DID YOU POOPIES?
I'M BACK ...
NO, AND I COULDN'T GO, ANY-WAYS.

I'M FINE.
とぷん
SPLOOSH
'CAUSE YOU...
WHEN I WENT CAMPING, THIS IS HOW WE MEASURED THE WATER.
...YOU CAN'T COOK, CAN YOU?
THAT'S FOR COOKING RICE OVER A CAMP-FIRE...

WE EAT ALL THE TIME.
IT'S BEEN A LONG TIME SINCE WE'VE EATEN!
Thanks!
Sure. Use this.
OR SHOULD I GO TO ANOTHER RESTAURANT?
MAYBE I SHOULD GO HOME.
Uhhh...
YOU NEED TO LET IT... ABSORB THE WATER, SO GIVE IT A MINUTE.
I'M GONNA DRAW WHILE WE WAIT!
FWIP
Hff
UM...
I MEAN TOGETHER, DADDY.
OH...

YOU MIGHT BE RIGHT...
YEAH ...
THAT SHOULD BE ENOUGH TIME... I THINK.
Umm...
SAKE!
I'VE HEARD IT TASTES BETTER IF YOU MIX IN A LITTLE SAKE.
I'M SURE OF IT.
MUMBLE
BLUP
BLUP
I'm nervous.
FWOOM
BEEP!
14 59
リセット
RESET
分
MIN
秒
SEC
START/STOP
スタート

すぴー
ZZZZZ
HISS
STEAMING
DA-DUM
It's not done yet.
DA-DUM
BLUB BLUB
FIDGET
FIDGET
"TSUMUGI!"
"YOU DON'T HAVE TO PUT SO MUCH EFFORT INTO IT EVERY TIME."
"KÔHEI-SAN! DINNER'S READY!"
"BUT YOU NEVER EAT ANYTHING!"
"I'M PUTTING MY SOUL INTO EVERY MEAL."
"I WANT YOU TO EAT SOMETHING GOOD."

ピピピッ
BEEP
BEEP
BEEP
BEEP
ビク…
TWITCH
Huh?
WAS I ASLEEP?
Yawn
ガば
KA-POP
もぐ
FWUF
わ、
WHUSH
ふぁ、
STEAM

Whew...
...READY!
THE RICE IS...
わっせ
わっせ
HERE WE GO!
OH, I'M SUPER-HUNGRY!
OKAY! EAT UP, EVERY-BODY!

LET'S EAT!
Just nice?!
MM... IT'S SO GOOD.
もぎゅ
CHEW
CHEW
もぎゅ
I CAN TASTE EVERY GRAIN.
ごくり
GULP
ISN'T IT AMAZING? IT'S THE FIRST TIME I'VE EVER—
Um, never mind.
ぱっ
CHOMP
はぐっ
CHOMP

WATCH ME EAT!
OH ...
DADDY, IT'S YUMMY!
IT'S SOOO YUMMY!
BA-DUM

WHAT'S WRONG?
NO.
I'M FINE.
...
WH...
IT'S NOTHING.
WHAT'S WRONG?
CHOMP はぐ
DADDY WILL EAT SOME, TOO.
TRY IT! 'KAY?
DELICIOUS.
SNIF ずっ
BA-DUM どき
BA-DUM どき
BA-DUM どき

O-OH!
UM...
TOPPINGS!
CLATTER
ガラン
OH!
I FOUND SOME PICKLED NOZAWANA AND MISO BEEF AND IWANORI SEAWEED!
PILE 'EM ON AND LET'S EAT!
MORE FOOD? MORE FOOD?
seconds
MUNCH
むち
TSU-MUGI.
MUNCH
むち
HMM?
I PROMISE YOU...

FROM NOW ON...
DADDY'S GONNA MAKE YOU GOOD FOOD LIKE THIS...
... SO LET'S EAT IT AND ENJOY IT TOGETHER.
REALLY ?!
WITH DADDY? I CAN EAT WITH DADDY?!
YUP! SURE THING!

W-
WAS MY RICE GOOD?
Oh...
YES.
THANK YOU.

UM, INU-ZUKA-SENSEI ...
YES?
I WANTED TO ASK YOU SOMETHING.
SENSEI?
Hm?

I'M...
I'M GOING TO BE...
...EATING DINNER ALONE MOST OF THE TIME FROM NOW ON.
SO...

WOULD YOU EAT WITH ME?
SENSEI!
COULD WE COOK AND EAT TOGETHER?
WHEN AM I GONNA GET MEAT AND STUFF?
はっ?
HUH?

DONABE RICE

☆ Ingredients ☆ Serves 3-4

1 1/2 cups rice
430 mL water – Try to have between 1.2 and 1.3 times as much water as rice.

A dash of sake

Steps

1. Wash the **rice**, then pour it and the **water** into the donabe. Cover and heat on medium high. When it seems ready to boil over, turn the heat to low and cook for 13 minutes.

POINT
Add a bit of flavor by putting in a little **sake**.

2. Turn the heat to high for 30 seconds, then turn off the heat and let it steam for ten minutes. Remove the lid and stir.

POINT
You can adjust the amount of water and the heat settings to your taste.

How to clean rice to make it delicious

Quickly!

1. Put the **rice** in a metal strainer. Soak the whole thing in a bowl filled with water. Stir the rice around with your hands and then lift it out of the water.

2. Continue to stir the **rice** without putting it back into the water. Stir it quickly but gently.

3. Get a fresh bowl of water and soak/mix again. Make sure the rice bran is getting rinsed off. Strain and stir. Repeat.

4. When the water no longer clouds up, strain the rice and let it sit for 30 minutes in the summer or an hour in the winter (to absorb the moisture).

I love rice!

This lets the rice fully aborb the water it's been soaked in.

CONVERSION NOTES:
430 ML WATER = ABOUT 1 3/4 CUPS

When we made rice at home, it boiled way over and scared us. Inaoka
(It was good though)
Waaah!
BLUB BLUB
Needs more research!
RUMBLE
RUMBLE

Chapter 2 Pork Miso Soup and Restaurant Lights

SLICE...
THE BUTTER'S HARD.
?
CRUMBLE
CRUMBLE
...
SPREAD
I SHOULD HAVE HUNG IN THERE AND JUST BOUGHT SOME...
Lettuce
There were too many different types, and I didn't know which was which!
Green
Romaine
I COULD REALLY USE SOME LETTUCE.
Well...
IT'S DONE!
...I GUESS.
MORNING...
Yawn
TSUMUGI! BREAKFAST!
WELL? IS IT GOOD?
IT TASTES LIKE THE STUFF IN IT...
CHOMP
I SEE...

THE REST ARE SO-SO.
I SEE.
THEN I'LL SEAL AWAY THE REST OF THEM.
AND I LIKE THIS ONE, TOO! IT'S SOFT AND YUMMY AND ROUND AND CUTE!
THIS ONE'S GOT AN ANIMAL PICTURE ON THE INSIDE, AND IT'S YUMMY.
OH, RIGHT. TSUMUGI!
ARE THERE ANY OF THESE YOU LIKE?
FOR BOXED LUNCHES?
PACKAGES: (L) EDAMAME VEGGIE MIX; (R) SHRIMP MACARONI CORN GRATIN, HOROSCOPE INCLUDED
SEAL THEM AWAY? WHY?
DADDY PROMISED YOU...
... THAT HE'D DO HIS BEST TO COOK FOR YOU, RIGHT?
THAT'S WHY.
FOOD...
WITH KOTORI-CHAN TOO?!
WELL...
MAYBE NOT...
I was thinking of taking a cooking class...

COULD WE COOK AND EAT TOGETHER?
HUH?
WHY?
DO YOU NOT WANT TO?
IT'S NOT ABOUT WHETHER I WANT TO OR NOT. I JUST CAN'T.

EATING DINNER WITH SOME RANDOM GUY AND HIS KID?
I DOUBT YOUR MOTHER WOULD BE OKAY WITH THAT. WE'D BE A BOTHER.
THAT'S NOT TRUE!
I'LL TALK TO MY MOM ABOUT IT!
THAT'S NOT THE ISSUE!
FOR ONE THING, WHY WOULD WE...
WHAT?
WHAT WHAT?
WHAT WHAT WHAT WHAT WHAAAT?
Tsu-
TSUMUGI, WAIT.
I WANT US TO ALL EAT HERE TOGETHER AGAIN.
REALLY?!
IT'S LIKE A RESTAURANT!
I WANNA DO THAT!

NO, NOT EVEN IF YOU MAKE A CUTE FACE!
Why? Why why?
Oh, jeez...

...

SO...
...THE RESTAURANT'S CLOSED A LOT, ANYWAY.

MY MOM WILL BE FINE, REALLY.
SHE'S BUSY WITH OTHER WORK NOW.

IT FEELS...
...LIKE THE RESTAURANT MIGHT SHUT DOWN.
...

IT DOESN'T HAVE TO BE EVERY DAY.
I DON'T HAVE A DAD...
...SO THERE'S NOBODY ELSE I CAN RELY ON.
JUST COME HERE ONCE IN A WHILE...
...TURN ON THE LIGHTS...
...AND MAKE SOMETHING TO EAT WITH ME.
HUH?
MY MOM WILL BE FINE WITH IT SINCE YOU'RE A TEACHER!
AND IT'S NOT LIKE WE DON'T KNOW YOU.
SO YOU ARE FROM MY SCHOOL...
YES.

HAVE YOU STILL NOT LEARNED THE NAMES OF YOUR STUDENTS?
YOU'RE MY ASSISTANT HOMEROOM TEACHER.
KOTORI IIDA, CLASS 1-A.
I'LL... GO HOME AND THINK ABOUT IT.
DING
DING
CLACK
FWIP
OKAY.
WHO CAN SOLVE THIS PROB-LEM?

I UNDERSTAND, SENSEI.
YOU DON'T WANT PEOPLE TO FIND OUT THAT YOU'RE MEETING WITH A FEMALE STUDENT OUTSIDE SCHOOL.
EATING HER SECOND BREAKFAST
MUNCH
MUNCH
I'LL PRETEND I DON'T KNOW ANYTHING SO PEOPLE DON'T MISUNDERSTAND.
GASP!
WHAT IF HE FALLS IN LOVE WITH ME?
?
BLUSH
SHAKE
SHAKE
...

IT WOULD BE BAD, RIGHT?
GOING TO A SPECIFIC STUDENT'S HOUSE...
HM... KOTORI IIDA, HUH?
HER DAD DIVORCED HER MOM WHEN SHE WAS IN THIRD GRADE.
I SEE.
HOMEROOM TEACHER: HOSAKA
BUT WHEN I WAS YOUNG, I WOULD GO HANG OUT WITH THE STUDENTS AND EAT AT THEIR HOUSES.
WELL...
...PEOPLE ARE MORE PARTICULAR ABOUT THAT LATELY.
SO NOT MANY TEACHERS INTERACT WITH STUDENTS OUTSIDE OF CLASS THESE DAYS.
WELL, IF YOU'RE TALKING TO ME ABOUT IT, YOU MUST NOT BE SURE WHAT TO DO.
PART OF YOU WANTS TO DO IT, RIGHT?
HM...
TRY TALKING WITH HER MOM. JUST ONCE.
Then you go, Sensei.
Nope. She's asking for you, right?
SHE CAN HELP YOU DECIDE WHAT TO DO.
WHETHER IT'S FOR YOUR LITTLE GIRL'S SAKE, OR FOR YOUR SAKE...

I DON'T KNOW WHICH, THOUGH...
TSUMUGI, YOU REALLY LIKE THAT PLACE, DON'T YOU?
PLUS, KOTORI-CHAN'S COOL!
IT'S KOTORI-CHAN'S HOUSE!
There's a whole story!?
...IS IT A PARK?
BZZT!
IT'S ME ENJOYING THE SALISBURY STEAK WITH EGG ON TOP THAT SHE WORKED SUPER HARD TO MAKE!
...
Whee!
TAP ぽち
ぽち TAP
BEEP ぴっ
THIS IS YOUR ASSISTANT HOMEROOM TEACHER, INUZUKA. I'D LIKE TO MEET YOUR MOTHER TO DISCUSS THE MATTER FROM THE OTHER DAY. PLEASE LET ME KNOW WHEN SHE HAS TIME. THANKS.
KÔHEI INUZUKA
YOU SEEMED TO GET ALONG WITH HER, TOO!

THIS WAY...
...I THINK.
THANK YOU. MY MOM WILL BE HERE WEDNESDAY NIGHT. PLEASE EAT WITH US. AND BRING TSUMUGI-CHAN!
CLASS 1-A KOTORI IIDA
OH DUH!
THAT WAS FAST.
CLATTER
EXCUSE ME...
THAT'S IT!
...SHE HAD TO LEAVE SUDDENLY FOR WORK.
She was here until this afternoon but...
Wait a second!
WHERE'S YOUR MOM?
IT'S TRUE! I HAVE A LETTER AND EVERY-THING!
AND I HAD HER PUT HER THUMB-PRINT ON IT, TOO!
Dear Inuzuka-sensei,
This is Kotori's mother.
I'm very grateful that
e're going to be looking
fter my daughter.
the kitchen however
you want. I'm sorry,
but I have to leave
suddenly for work.
Thank you very much.
: Iida
WOW ...
EXTREMELY SORRY

WOULD YOU AT LEAST STAY AND EAT WITH ME?
I'VE GOT ALL THE INGREDI-ENTS, TOO.
I'M BRIBING HER WITH ONE OF MY OLD APRONS.
She said I could have this!
LOOK, DADDY!
!!
So cute...
THAT'S NOT THE PROBLEM!
WOULD IT BE BETTER IF SHE HAD SIGNED IT IN BLOOD?
~~~~...
JUST FOR TODAY, OKAY?
OKAY!
~~~~

OKAY, THEN.
WHAT SHOULD WE DO?
THE PLAN WAS FOR YOUR MOM TO MAKE US SALISBURY STEAK FROM SCRATCH, BUT...
DON'T WORRY.
I HAD HER WRITE DOWN THE RECIPE FOR ME.

FROM THE LOOKS OF IT...
Hm?
LET ME SEE.
SALISBURY
It's easy
Step 1
Slice up the onions into tiny bits!
You'll cry a bit.
cook until they change color.
cooking yay!
SUPER-SIMPLE
OH.

IS THIS A PICTURE BOOK?
I TOLD HER THERE'D BE A LITTLE GIRL COMING...
... SO SHE MADE IT KIND OF KID-FRIENDLY.

YOU REALLY DON'T EAT A LOT, SENSEI.
IF WE COULD AT LEAST DO THE SALISBURY STEAK...
THAT WAS TSUMUGI-CHAN'S REQUEST, WASN'T IT?
I see that now.

...ALSO, WE CAN'T POSSIBLY EAT ALL THIS.
MENU
Rice
Miso Soup
Salisbury Steak with
Dressing
Potatoes
Ice Cream
WHAT ?!
A menu featuring everybody's requests.

THAT'S FINE FOR THE MAIN DISH...
...BUT I STILL WANT PORK MISO SOUP.
SO LET'S MAKE IT!
IRON POT
DO YOU PUT POTATOES IN MISO SOUP?
WE DO AT MY HOUSE!
Although in the winter we use taro.
YOU PUT ALL THAT IN?
YES!
SWISH
SWISH
WOW!
I LIKE TO PUT IN A LOT OF MEAT AND VEGETA-BLES.
SNOW PEAS
FRIED TOFU
DAIKON
KOZZUKUKI
PORK BUTT
POTATOES
CARROTS
BURDOCK
GREEN ONION
AND THE STEAK ...?
WE'LL GET THIS DONE AHEAD OF TIME AND THEN MAKE THE STEAK!
Otherwise it'll get cold!
Okay, Sensei.
WASH YOUR HANDS AND CUT THE VEGETABLES!

Ummm...
DO I CUT THE DAIKON RADISH FIRST?
I'M GLAD SHE DREW THOSE PIC-TURES NOW.
FINGERS IN LIKE A CAT'S PAW...
LIKE A CAT'S PAW...
CHOP!
CAN I REALLY HAVE THIS?
ぱっし
CATCH
Yeah
IT'S A PRESENT FOR YOU.
SHIIK
SHIIK
CHOP
CHOP
THUMP
THUMP
THUMP

しゃく
SLICE
SLICE しゃく
SLICE しゃく
OOH...
HUH?
UM...
YES?
WHY ARE YOU SITTING THERE?
IF WE DON'T DO THIS TOGETHER, WE'LL BE HERE ALL NIGHT.
My arms are starting to shake...
Oh
I'M THE TASTE TESTER.
TASTE TESTER?
Oh!
SENSEI! IF YOU DON'T CUT ALL THE PIECES INTO THE SAME SIZE...
... THEY'LL ABSORB THE FLAVOR UNEVENLY.

SO...
YOU CAN'T COOK EITHER, RIGHT?
OR SO I'VE HEARD.

SWF
...WHY DON'T YOU CUT THEM WITH ME?

I'M...
...THE TASTE TESTER.

I...

OKAY...
...THAT'S FINE.
...
DID I ASK HER IN A BAD WAY?
CHOP
ドェり
How is it?

WHAT ABOUT YOU?
TEARING IT APART LOOKS LIKE IT'LL BE FUN.
OK
YOU TEAR THE KONNYAKU APART AND PARBOIL IT TO REDUCE BITTERNESS AND SOFTEN IT UP.
TSUMUGI, CAN YOU HELP ME?
PACKAGE: KONNYAKU
...
Like this?
ぶちっ
RIP
Like this, Tsumugi. Like this.
I'M NO GOOD AT COOKING EITHER...
...BUT THERE'S NOTHING EMBARRASSING ABOUT NOT BEING ABLE TO DO SOMETHING.
I...

I'M SCARED ...
...OF KNIVES.
WHEN I WAS LITTLE ...
...I CUT MYSELF REALLY BADLY.
I'M SORRY.
KNIVES SCARE ME.
OH, I SEE...

SO YOU WANTED SOMEONE TO DO THE CUTTING FOR YOU?
Unngh
...
YES.
YOU WERE HAVING TROUBLE, AND I LIKE TO EAT, AND I CAN BE A TASTE TESTER...
I THOUGHT IT WAS A REALLY GOOD IDEA, BUT..
I WISH I COULD DO IT.
MY MOM'S ALWAYS BUSY, AND I KNOW IT WOULD HELP HER.
BUT I JUST CAN'T.

ACTUALLY, I FEEL BETTER NOW THAT I KNOW WHAT YOU WERE THINKING.
...?
OH.
NO.
I'M SORRY I DIDN'T TELL YOU.
I WASN'T TRYING TO USE YOU OR ANY-THING.
BUT IT LOOKS LIKE I WAS...
I WAS REALLY IN A BIND.
I DIDN'T KNOW IF I COULD MAKE GOOD FOOD FOR TSUMUGI BY MYSELF.
IT'S TOUGH.
FOR BOTH OF US...
SO IN A WAY...
...COOKING TOGETHER IS GOOD FOR BOTH OF US.
...AND WHEN WE SAW THE LIGHTS ON HERE, WE FELT SO RELIEVED.
I KNOW YOU DON'T WANT THE RESTAU-RANT TO CLOSE...

BUNNY!
IT'S GOOD FOR ME IF TSUMUGI'S WISH COMES TRUE.
THAT'S RIGHT.
THERE'S A CAT, TOO!
Meow!
Oh!
IT SHOULD HAVE BEEN BOILED.
CAN I EAT THIS?
THIS ONE!
CAN I USE THIS ONE?!
WOW!
THIS ONE!

DADDY! MAKE IT THINNER!
SURE THING.
GARRR
Uuuugh... This carrot...
IS IT STILL A LITTLE TOO TOUGH?
LET'S PARBOIL IT.
WHAT ABOUT THE MEAT?
...OR SO I'VE HEARD.
IT BRINGS OUT THE FLAVOR.
YOU BOIL THE WATER FIRST, RIGHT?
PAPER: TSU TSU TSU... MU MU MU...
TABLE: KOTORI IIDA

HUH?
NOW IT'S YOUR TURN.
...REALLY MAKES YOUR SHOULDERS STIFF, HUH...
KRIK KRIK
Sigh...
COOKING...
Ha ha
BUBBLE
くつくつ……
H-hey!
Hee.
TSUMUGI MAKES THE MENU!
DADDY CUTS!
KOTORI-CHAN TASTES!
STICK
Hey! Hey!
BRING ME TAPE!
ALSO...
...PLEASE TASTE IT.
IS IT OKAY IF WE TAPE IT UP?
WE'LL TAKE IT DOWN BEFORE WE GO HOME.
YES, IT'S FINE.
WHISPER
SEASONING IS WHAT I'M WORST AT.

WILL YOU HELP ME?
FOR TSU-MUGI, TOO.
YES ...

SOME PEOPLE LIKE STRONG FLAVORS.
SOME PREFER MILD ONES.
IT'S FINE TO LEARN TO PUT IN A SPECIFIC AMOUNT...
...BUT I LIKE ADDING THE FLAVOR LITTLE BY LITTLE.
みそ
JAR: MISO

YOU LEARNED YOUR MOTHER'S WAY OF SEASONING, HUH?
...
I LIKE ABOUT THIS MUCH!
Heh heh
HOW IS IT?

...IT'S DELICIOUS.
Let's eaaat!
PUFF はっ
PUFF ふっ
PUFF はっ
SSSLURP
BA-DUM
BA-DUM
BA-DUM

MM...
PUFF
は
IT'S SOOO GOOD!
COLLAPSE
カクー!!
Whoa!
SENSEI?

I'M FINE.
I'M JUST SO INCREDIBLY HAPPY, YOU KNOW?
YEAH ...
THE POTATOES ARE PRETTY GOOD.
RIGHT? SO HOT AND TASTY! TARO ARE BEST IN WINTER, BUT I ALSO LIKE YAMS AND SWEET POTATOES.
CHOMP もぐ
Look, my star!
Hmpwh!
IT'S HA'!
THE PO'A'OES AH HA'!
PUFF
BLOW ON THEM.
PUFF

BUT WE RAN OUT OF ENERGY AND NEVER MADE THE SALISBURY STEAK...
I'm glad the rice was done in time.
Sorry-
Ahh...
BUT RICE AND PORK MISO SOUP...
...GO TOGETHER SO WONDERFULLY.
HAPPY
Sweet! Yummy yummy!

YEAH!
LOOKING FORWARD TO NEXT TIME!
Hee hee!

LET'S DO SALISBURY STEAK NEXT TIME!
SALISBURY STEAK AND RICE OMELETTES, AND THAT MEATBALL THING WOULD BE GOOD, TOO!

...OKAY.

I NEED TO GET TSUMUGI READY FOR BED.
WE'LL BE LEAVING AT EIGHT.

...

YOU TOO, KOTORI-CHAN!
...
I...

BOW
LET'S DO THIS AGAIN SOON.
I WANTED TO FIGURE A BUNCH OF OTHER THINGS OUT...
...BUT WE CAN DO THAT NEXT TIME.
I HAD FUN RUNNING AROUND THE KITCHEN MAKING FOOD WITH YOU.
HUH?
AND SO DID TSUMUGI. SO...
HUH?
PAPER: SEA, SQUID
LOOKING FORWARD TO IT!
O-OKAY!

MISO PORK SOUP

☆ Ingredients ☆ Serves 3-4

- 7 cm daikon radish
- 1/2 carrot
- 1/2 green onion
- 1/3 burdock root
- 1 potato
- 150 g pork (brisket)
- 1/2 block konnyaku
- 9 snow pea pods
- 1 pouch fried tofu
- 1 Tbsp sesame oil
- 800 mL dashi stock
- 4 Tbsp miso

1. Cut the **carrots** and **daikon radish** into quarter rounds, then cut the **green onion** into 1 cm slices. Chop the **burdock root** in thin diagonal slices and place in cold water. Cut the **potatoes** and **pork** into bite-sized pieces. Tear the **konnyaku** into bite-sized chunks and then parboil. Parboil the **snow peas** and the **fried tofu**. Drain.

2. Put the **sesame oil** into the pot and stir-fry the **pork** on medium heat. Add and fry the ingredients in this order: **carrots**, **burdock root**, **daikon radish**, **potatoes**, **konnyaku**. Once the edges of the **potatoes** become translucent, add in the **dashi stock**.

POINT: You can boil the ingredients instead of frying. The taste will be lighter.

3. Once it starts boiling, skim off the scum that forms on top. Simmer on low heat for 7-8 minutes, then add the **green onion** and **fried tofu**.

4. Once the ingredients are softened, add the **miso** by dissolving it gradually into the stock. Once it starts boiling again, immediately turn off the heat and add the **snow peas**.

CONVERSION NOTES:
7 CM DAIKON = 3 IN., 150 G PORK = ABOUT 5 1/4 OZ, 800 ML DASHI = ABOUT 3 1/3 CUPS

The third bowl tastes best poured over rice.
Third...?!
Is it good?

Chapter 3 Tsumugi and the Long-Awaited Salisbury Steak

Hnn...
BEEP
BEEP
BEEP
BEEP
BEEP
BEEP
ピ
ピ
ピ
ピ
ピ
ピ
STEP
STEP
STEP
STEP
CLICK
トー
STEP
mumble
mumble
MORNING ...
CLICK
しん
SILENCE
トー
STEP

WOW!
SPARKLE
しゅ
ガ
To Kotori
- From Mom
WOW...

WOW!
MY FRIED TOFU IS SO LONG!
DANGLE
HOW'S THE MISO SOUP? I ACCIDENTALLY BOILED IT A LITTLE...
BUT I FLAVORED IT LIKE WE DID WITH THE PORK MISO SOUP...
YOURS IS ALL BURNT, DADDY!
I HAVE TO PAY FOR MY MISTAKES.

CONGRATULATIONS.
Let's look at the weather...
BEEP
REALLY ?!
IS THAT A THING?!
!?!
THAT MEANS YOU, UH...
...WON, TSUMUGI.

BEEP
ぱ
FLICK
A LIVE BROADCAST?
Good morning! Mommy's got a live broadcast at 7:15 this morning. Nervous. Have a good vacation!
HM?
RUSTLE
What's this?
7:15...?
Huh?
RIGHT NOW?

BE SURE TO WATCH!
A TWO HOUR SPECIAL, TONIGHT AT 7!
Quiz Academy KnowKnow
SO TONIGHT AT SEVEN, IT'S THE QUIZ ACADEMY KNOWKNOW SPECIAL! WITH SPECIAL GUEST...
...COOKING RESEARCHER MEGUMI IIDA!
We're here with the two guys from High-Low PD and Taka Megu-san!
?!
Ha ha ha!
Uh,
IIDA-SAN, PLEASE STICK TO THE SCRIPT.
YAAAY!
KOTORIIII! YOU WATCHING? YOUR MOM'S GONNA DO HER BEST!

...AND MY MOM WAS WEARING A SAILOR UNIFORM.
I TURNED ON THE TV IN THE MORNING...
CHOMP
ぱく
EVEN IF IT IS FOR TV, THERE ARE SOME THINGS YOU SHOULDN'T DO!
NO WAY.
I MEAN, JUST, NO WAY!
ぱく
CHOMP
SO IS THIS WHY YOUR MOM IS BUSY?
YEAH.
IT'S NOT LIKE SHE'S REALLY BECOME A CELEBRITY, THOUGH.
IS THAT THE PROBLEM?
I'VE NEVER EVEN WORN A SAILOR UNIFORM!
And it looked great on her.

...I BURNED THE SCRAMBLED EGGS.
OH...
OH.
HMM?
HOW WAS BREAKFAST, BY THE WAY?
BUT YOU WERE ABLE TO MAKE THE MISO SOUP, RIGHT?
Oh...
You made the pork miso already.
AFTER I PUT IN THE MISO, I PUT THE HEAT ON A LITTLE...
...AND IT BOILED DOWN, SO I ADDED MORE HOT WATER...
...I SEE.
Huh?
Hmm...
SENSEI, ARE YOU AFRAID OF FOOD NOT BEING COOKED ALL THE WAY?
ざわ
MURMUR
ざわ
MURMUR

WHY? WHAT'RE YOU DOING?
HUH?
MAKING SALISBURY STEAK!
TSUMUGI-CHAN!
LET'S PLAY!
LATER!
Busy!
Busy!
THIS IS...
...FOR DADDY!
SLAM
YOU CAN USE MINE.
MINE, TOO.
REALLY?! IT'S OKAY?
SURE. WE HAVEN'T USED OUR CLAY LATELY.
I MADE ONE, BUT NOW I DON'T HAVE CLAY TO MAKE A PLATE OR CHOPSTICKS OR A SPOON.
Oh...
OH NO ...

TSUMUGI-CHAN, YOU'RE COMING TO PLAY OVER AT MY PLACE TODAY, RIGHT?
I can't wait!
YEAH! DADDY SAYS THANK YOU!
YOUR PARENTS WILL BE HERE SOON!
EVERY-ONE!
Let's clean up, okay?
OKAY!
...
THANK YOU!!
It's fine!
It's fine!
HUH?
YUP!
ARE YOU TAKING THAT?
PILED HIGH
TS...
TSU-MUGI-CHAN...
BOX: TSUMUGI INUZUKA, CLAY
HEY!
THAT'S NOT FAIR!
OH! THEY GAVE IT TO ME!
OH MY.
WHAT'S ALL THAT CLAY?

BUT IT'S NOT FAIR SHE GETS IT ALL FOR HERSELF!
YEAH ...
RIGHT ?
NUH-UH! THEY GAVE IT TO ME!
SHE'S TAKING OTHER PEOPLE'S CLAY!
SENSEI!
WOW, SO YOU'RE NOT GIVING IT BACK?
THEY GAVE IT TO ME, SO IT'S MINE NOW!
THAT'S WHAT WE CALL A THIEF!

Easy RECIPE Search!
SENSEI.
YES?
トッキ JUMP
Heh heh...
DID SOMETHING GOOD HAPPEN?
Huh?
NO, WHY?
WELL, IT JUST SEEMED LIKE IT.
I SEE...
RING RING RING
Oh!
YES? THIS IS INUZUKA.
YES...
HUH?
YES.
OH...
SORRY. I'LL COME GET HER.
BEEP
IS SOMETHING WRONG?
OH.

TSU-MUGI!
THERE'S BEEN A LITTLE TROUBLE WITH MY DAUGHTER.
Oh, gotcha.
Sure. Get going.
I'll tell the vice-principal.
SO, UH...
TSUMUGI AND MIKIO-KUN ARE...
INUZUKA-SAN, SORRY TO CALL YOU LIKE THIS.
NO, IT'S OKAY. THANK YOU.
TSU...
I DID NOT!
TSUMUGI-CHAN SCRATCHED ME!
A tiny bit.
...OVER THERE.

TSUMUGI, DID YOU ACCIDENTALLY HIT HIM?
I DIDN'T DO IT!
MIKIO-KUN, YOU PUSHED HER AND HER HAND SCRATCHED YOU.
That must've hurt, huh?
BUT SHE STILL DID IT!
IT WASN'T ON PURPOSE. I SAW.
JERK
BAM
MIKIO!
UH...
HMM...
SO YOU PUSHED HER FIRST, RIGHT? THEN YOU NEED TO APOLOGIZE!
I... I PUSHED HER AND WHEN SHE FELL BACK SHE GRABBED OUT AND SCRATCHED ME...
THEY SAID YOU MADE A GIRL CRY AGAIN!
NO... I DIDN'T...
Please calm down.
SO WHAT HAPPENED?!
COME ON, LIKE YOU MEAN IT! MAKE UP WITH HER!
I...
I'M SORRY...

NO WAY!

NEVER!!

BOW
See you!
Bye bye, Tsumugi-chan!
YEAH.
SORRY.
CAN I TAKE HER HOME AND TALK WITH HER?
...
DING
VNNN
HEY, TSU-MUGI.
IT'S JUST DADDY NOW.

THEY GAVE ME THE CLAY...
I'M NOT A THIEF.
I KNOW. YOU'RE NOT A THIEF, TSUMUGI.
HE SAID A MEAN THING TO YOU, DIDN'T HE?
YEAH.
HEY. WHY DON'T WE BUY SOME CLAY AT HOME SO YOU CAN GIVE THEIRS BACK?
WHY?
TO SORT THINGS OUT.
DADDY DOESN'T WANT YOU TO BE CALLED A THIEF, EITHER, EVEN IF IT'S A MISUNDER-STANDING.
...
...OKAY.
THERE, THERE.
PAT PAT

SO...
...I WAS HOPING TO CHEER HER UP WITH THE SALISBURY STEAK.
OKAY.
LET'S DO OUR BEST.
...S-sorry, okay?
Sorry.
Glance
Glance
...BUT SHE DOESN'T SEEM TO FEEL BETTER.
YES... THEY DID MAKE UP THIS MORNING...
Sigh
I SEE.
SO THAT'S WHY SHE'S SO DEPRESSED.
The next day
TSUMUGI-CHAN!
IT'S TIME FOR YOUR LONG-AWAITED SALIS-BURY STEAK!
OH... IT'S REALLY BAD.
コクリ
DROOP

IT'S HARD TO GET THE TEMPERATURE RIGHT ON SALISBURY STEAK, RIGHT?
OH... ABOUT THAT.
LET'S STEW IT!
WE'LL MAKE STEWED SALISBURY STEAK!
SO NOW, SENSEI...
...I'M GOING TO HAVE YOU MINCE THE ONIONS!
YOU DON'T HAVE TO WORRY ABOUT UNDERCOOKING THE MIDDLE!
AND IT TASTES GOOD!
THUD
ONIONS
BREADCRUMBS
THUD
GROUND BEEF
GROUND PORK
OH, I SEE.

WHAT IS THIS?
They fit over my glasses, but...
APPARENTLY, YOUR EYES WILL REALLY STING.
OKAY, TIME TO...
TIME TO...
LOOK, SHE'S LAUGHING A LITTLE.
You're right.
UH, HOW DO YOU MINCE ONIONS, EXACTLY?
I DON'T KNOW IF IT'LL HELP, BUT...
Oh...
...I HAD MY MOM WRITE ME INSTRUCTIONS.
IT'S NOT REALLY OBVIOUS TO FOLLOW, BUT...
Heh...
Cut in half
Slice horizontally
Leave this part
Then vertically
Spin it around
Cut from above, and it'll be chopped!
Hold down the tip of the knife with your fingers
and cut into tiny bits
It's easy!
I DON'T THINK I CAN DO THIS...

UM...
I REALLY DON'T HAVE MUCH CONFIDENCE TODAY...
...SO IT MIGHT BE BETTER IF YOU DON'T WATCH ME GET HURT.
AH!
YES!
SORRY!
ANXIOUS
はら
はら
ANXIOUS
BUT...
...I'LL DO IT ANYWAY.
SLICE
SLICE
UM...
I'VE GOT LOTS OF BANDAGES, OKAY?

OKAY!
FRY THEM UNTIL THEY GET SORTA CARAMEL-IZED.
TAP トン
TAP トン
WHAT DOES THAT MEAN?
WELL, WE WON'T TOTALLY CARAMELIZE THEM, BUT THEY'LL GET TRANSLUCENT BROWN AND YUMMY!
GOOD... I DIDN'T NEED THE BAND-AIDS.
じゅっ
SIZZLE

SO...
...YOU SOAK THE BREAD-CRUMBS IN MILK?
HUH...
THERE ARE FEWER INGREDIENTS IN THIS THAN I THOUGHT.
IT TASTES REALLY GOOD...
...BUT IT'S BASICALLY A SIMPLE DISH.
Then again...
SOME PEOPLE PUT SOY PULP OR TOFU OR KIWI INTO IT.
OH, NOW.
HEY!
TSUMUGI, WANNA HELP?
WE'RE GOING TO MAKE THE PATTIES FOR THE MEAT.
YOU LIKE CLAY, RIGHT?
HEY...
WHAT WOULD CHEER YOU UP, TSUMUGI?
NO...

I TOLD YOU THAT, RIGHT?
I KNOW YOU'RE NOT A THIEF.
YOU CAN'T.
'CAUSE YOU THINK I DID SOME-THING BAD!
BUT...
THAT'S NOT IT.
THAT'S NOT IT...
SQUEEZE...
IT'S...
...REALLY HARD TO TELL YOUR PAR-ENTS...
...WHEN YOU THINK YOU'VE DONE SOMETHING WRONG, RIGHT?
WHAT IS IT?
SHF
SENSEI, TRY ASKING HER AGAIN, HARDER.

TSU-MUGI?
I'M NOT A THIEF...
BUT THEY GAVE ME A LOT OF CLAY...
...AND I DIDN'T GIVE IT BACK.
SO...
...DOES THAT MAKE ME A BAD GIRL?
Huh?

TSUMUGI!
YOU'RE NOT A BAD GIRL!
EVEN IF YOU DID THE WRONG THING BY ACCIDENT, I STILL LOVE YOU!
I'LL LOVE YOU, NO MATTER WHAT KIND OF GIRL YOU ARE!

HEE HEE.

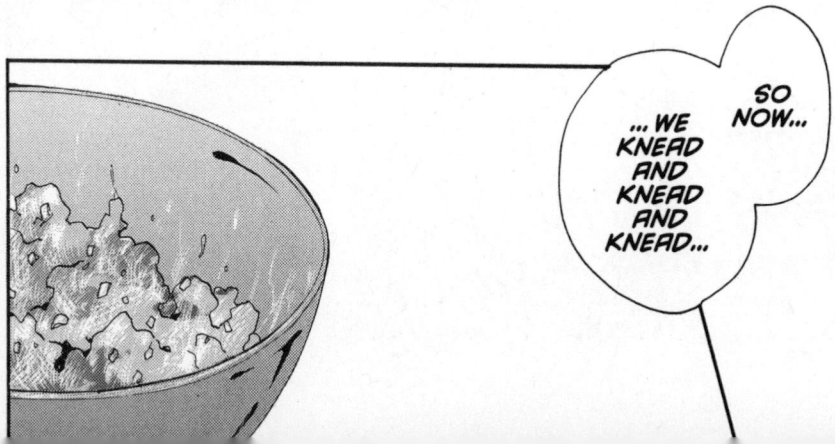
SO NOW...
... WE KNEAD AND KNEAD AND KNEAD...

コクリ。
NOD
OKAY! COME ON, TSUMUGI!
MMPH!
ぱちんっ
SLAP
AND THEN FORM IT INTO A PATTY LIKE SO...
ぱちん、
SLAP
... WHILE GETTING THE AIR OUT.
ぱ
SMACK!
んっ

SIZZLE
じゅわっ
We're stewing it after it's fried, so it just needs to change color!
Hmm...
Is the other side cooking, too?
STEAM
Carefully...
STEAM
Carefully...
Crumble a bouillon cube with your fingers...
DROP
DROP
Ooh!
We can make a simple sauce with canned tomatoes as the base!
Let's add ketchup and tonkatsu sauce!

IT'S...
IT'S DONE!

MM...

GULP
ブーン!
There's even an egg...
THIS IS THE BEST-LOOKING THING WE'VE MADE YET.
HERE YOU GO, TSUMUGI! LET'S EAT!
Ooh...

TSU-MUGI.
YOUR HAIR.
はCHOMP

IT'S GOOD...
DRIP
ぽ
ろ
ろ
WAAAHH!
DADDY...!
W...
Waah!
W...
W...
W...
W...
TSU-MU...
Daaaad-dyyyyy!
TSU-MUGI...
...YOU'VE ALWAYS, ALWAYS BEEN A GOOD GIRL.
Waaah!

IT'S ANOTHER BIG SUCCESS!
It's...
HEY! WE'RE PRETTY GOOD AT THIS, AREN'T WE?
It's good!
IT'S SO LIGHT AND FLUFFY!
Hee
I'M GLAD.
YUP.
Hee hee hee!
I'M SORRY.
DADDY'S BIRTHDAY PRESENT!
WHAT WERE YOU TRYING TO MAKE WITH ALL THAT CLAY, TSUMUGI-CHAN?
OH, RIGHT!

Chapter 3 - END

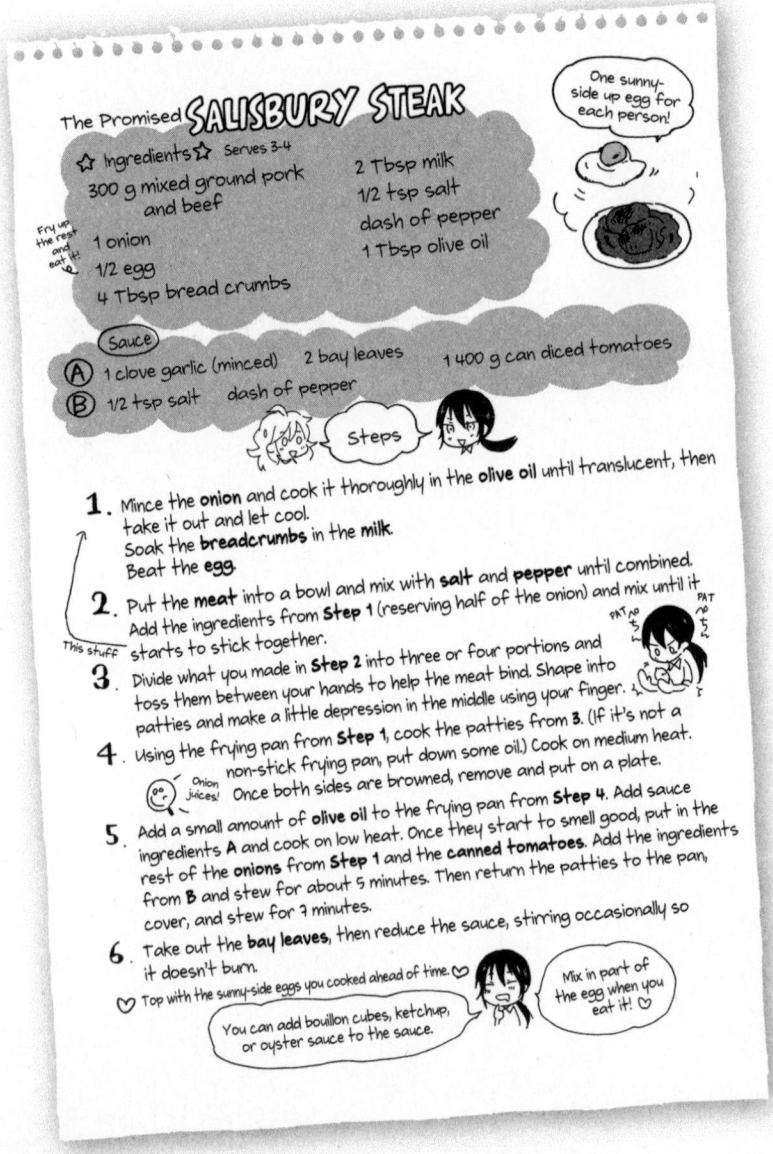

The Promised **SALISBURY STEAK**

One sunny-side up egg for each person!

☆ Ingredients ☆ Serves 3-4

300 g mixed ground pork and beef
1 onion
1/2 egg
4 Tbsp bread crumbs
2 Tbsp milk
1/2 tsp salt
dash of pepper
1 Tbsp olive oil

Fry up the rest and eat it!

Sauce

Ⓐ 1 clove garlic (minced) 2 bay leaves 1 400 g can diced tomatoes

Ⓑ 1/2 tsp salt dash of pepper

Steps

1. Mince the **onion** and cook it thoroughly in the **olive oil** until translucent, then take it out and let cool.
   Soak the **breadcrumbs** in the **milk**.
   Beat the **egg**.
2. Put the **meat** into a bowl and mix with **salt** and **pepper** until combined. Add the ingredients from **Step 1** (reserving half of the onion) and mix until it starts to stick together.

   This stuff

   PAT PAT
3. Divide what you made in **Step 2** into three or four portions and toss them between your hands to help the meat bind. Shape into patties and make a little depression in the middle using your finger.
4. Using the frying pan from **Step 1**, cook the patties from **3**. (If it's not a non-stick frying pan, put down some oil.) Cook on medium heat. Once both sides are browned, remove and put on a plate.

   Onion juices!
5. Add a small amount of **olive oil** to the frying pan from **Step 4**. Add sauce ingredients **A** and cook on low heat. Once they start to smell good, put in the rest of the **onions** from **Step 1** and the **canned tomatoes**. Add the ingredients from **B** and stew for about 5 minutes. Then return the patties to the pan, cover, and stew for 7 minutes.
6. Take out the **bay leaves**, then reduce the sauce, stirring occasionally so it doesn't burn.

♡ Top with the sunny-side eggs you cooked ahead of time. ♡

You can add bouillon cubes, ketchup, or oyster sauce to the sauce.

Mix in part of the egg when you eat it! ♡

CONVERSION NOTES:
300 G PORK AND BEEF = ABOUT 10 1/2 OZ, 400G TOMATOES = ABOUT 1 14.5 OZ CAN

Hey...
The meat...
...was so yummy, wasn't it?
Tsumugi...
Yeah...
...let's go to bed...
...okay...?
It was so juicy...
...wasn't it?

ARE YOU GOING SOME-WHERE FOR GOLDEN WEEK?
LET'S GO SEE A MOVIE!
MUR.MUR
WE'RE GOING TO DISMEY.
MUR.MUR
COME OVER TO MY PLACE!
MUR.MUR
GOLDEN WEEK, HUH? I USED TO GO ON TRIPS AND STUFF.
Hmm.
ARE YOU GOING ANYWHERE WITH YOUR DAUGHTER, INUZUKA-SENSEI?
I'VE GOT CLUB ACTIVITIES EVERY DAY!
BAM
...I THINK I'LL BE TAKING WORK HOME, BUT I'M TAKING THE WHOLE DAY OFF ON THE FIFTH TO HAVE FUN.
JUMP
FOR GOLDEN WEEK...
... WE'RE GOING ON A PICNIC!

Chapter 4 Golden Week and Packed Lunches

ARE YOU GUYS GOING ON A PICNIC TOO, SENSEI?
YEAH. WE'RE GOING TO A NATURE PARK BY CAR.
WE'LL EAT A PACKED LUNCH... ...AND JUST RELAX AND HAVE FUN.
WAIT. ARE YOU GOING ON ONE, TOO?
YUP!
I'M TAKING A LUNCH AND GOING ON A PICNIC WITH MY MOM!
WE'LL BOTH BE DOING THE SAME THING!
UM, SO... WOULD YOU MIND COOKING WITH ME?
I... I WAS JUST ABOUT TO ASK YOU THE SAME THING!

GOOD MORNING!
GOOD MORNING!
And so...
SORRY TO COME SO EARLY.
These are the ingredi-ents.
NO, IT'S TOTALLY FINE!
SHAKE
SHAKE
LET'S WORK TOGETHER AND MAKE...
...A LUNCH FILLED WITH STUFF!
GOOD MORNING!

IN THAT TIME, WE'RE GOING TO MAKE ONIGIRI, FRIED CHICKEN, TAMAGOYAKI, CABBAGE AND SHIRASU STIR-FRY, MARINATED VEGETABLES, HAM SKEWERS, CHIKUWA STUFFED WITH CUCUMBER AND CHEESE, AND SQUASH AND CREAM CHEESE!
WE'VE GOT ABOUT THREE HOURS UNTIL YOU GUYS LEAVE AND I MEET WITH MY MOM.
LET'S DO OUR BEST!
UH...
All that?
CUCUMBERS
THE WHAT NOW?
TURNIPS
CARROTS
OKAY, FOR STARTERS...
...LET'S MAKE THE MARINATED (?) VEGGIE THINGIES.
CELERY
LETTUCE
YOU SOAK WHATEVER VEGGIES YOU LIKE IN SWEET 'N' SOUR STUFF.
THIS IS MY CHANCE TO MAKE UP FOR WHEN SHE SKIPPED OUT ON FLOWER-VIEWING!
OF COURSE!
YOU'RE REALLY FIRED UP!
YOU WATCH US!
WHAT DO I DO?

...IF I MAKE A REALLY DELICIOUS LUNCH, SHE'LL BE SO SURPRISED!
SO...
YOUR MOM'S REALLY BUSY, ISN'T SHE?
THAT'S RIGHT. I HAVEN'T HAD TIME TO REALLY TALK TO HER LATELY.
I can't show her how much better I've gotten at cooking.
YOU'RE RIGHT.
SHE WILL BE SURPRISED.
I BET SHE'LL BE REALLY HAPPY.

SHE'S CLOSE WITH HER MOM.
ぱた FLIP
AND NEXT...
THEN THE CARROTS. THEN YOU ADD SALT TO MAKE THEM SOFT.
...WE SLICE THE TURNIPS.
SO...
SLICE
SLICE.
ぱた FLIP
HERE'S THE SLICER!
LET'S DO OUR BEST, SENSEI!
OK-OU!
THRUST!
Like this, maybe?
SHE MAY LOOK LIKE SHE HAS IT TOGETHER, BUT...
I BET THAT JUST...
...MAKES HER LONELIER.
...
SLICE
...
SHE'S REALLY JUST THROWING STUFF IN THERE.
AND MAYBE A LITTLE SALT OR SOY SAUCE...
Hmm?
LICK
LET'S DO OLIVE OIL, LEMON JUICE, AND VINEGAR FOR THE DRESSING.
Umm...
CHILL!
どわ
R-RIGHT!
YOU'LL CUT YOUR FINGER ON THE SLICER, SENSEI.
DON'T SPACE OUT.

FRIED CHICKEN?
AND NOW WE START THE FRIED CHICKEN...
SLAM
THEN WE DRAIN AND MARINATE THE VEGETABLES.
IF YOU DON'T MIND, WRITE DOWN WHAT YOU PUT IN AND HOW MUCH.
I'M TASTE-TESTING EVERYTHING, OKAY?
So we can make it again later.
Wow.
FRIED CHICKEN!
FRIED CHICKEN!
LET'S EAT IT!
THE FRIED CHICKEN?
I LOVE FRIED CHICKEN!
YES. WE MARINATE IT IN A SAUCE WITH GARLIC, GRATED GINGER, SAKE, AND LOTS OF SOY SAUCE, AND THEN...
ONCE IT SOAKS UP THE FLAVOR, WE FRY IT!
WOOOOW
W-WE'RE MAKING THE FRIED CHICKEN LATER...
Huff
Huff
I WANNA MAKE FRIED CHICKEN, TOO!
But I wanna... but I wanna!
Uhh...
Right, right.

CAN YOU MAKE THE HAM AND CARROTS 'N' STUFF INTO STARS WITH THIS?
HMMMM?
OKAY, TSUMUGI.

WOW!
They sell all kinds of cute ones.
YOU CAN LAYER VEGGIES WITH HAM OR WHATEVER AND THEN STICK A TOOTHPICK THROUGH THEM TO MAKE THEM CUTE!

YES!!
YOU'RE THE GIRL FOR THE JOB!
WE'RE COUNTING ON YOU!
YAY!
I DID THAT LAST TIME!
OH, THAT...
GRIN

UM... COAT THE PAN WITH SESAME OIL, TOSS IN THE CABBAGE AND SHIRASU...
BUSY
OH, THIS! LET'S MAKE THIS!
UMM... UM...
UM...!
WE NEED TO LET THE FRIED CHICKEN MARINATE.
Pace
The rice isn't quite done yet...
BUSY
It needs to absorb water.
Pace
For a little under an hour, maybe?

CABBAGE AND SHIRASU STIR-FRY
DONABE RICE WITH KONBU STOCK
MICRO-WAVED SQUASH WITH CREAM CHEESE
CHIKUWA STUFFED WITH CUCUMBER AND CHEESE
WOULDN'T IT HAVE BEEN EASIER TO CUT THE CHIKUWA AFTER WE PUT THIS STUFF IN?
Oh!
HAM AND VEGGIE STACKS (WITH MAYO)

WHEW

UNTIL NOW, WE'VE BEEN CUTTING, MIXING, AND OCCASIONALLY SAUTEEING THINGS...
...WHICH IS STUFF WE CAN DO AT OUR LEVEL.
BUT... FRIED STUFF IS AT THE TOP OF THE PYRAMID, ISN'T IT?
I know!
Slicing fish and stuff
Frying things
Hard
Ingredients you've never heard of
Seasonal stuff
Easy
Microwaving
Just add hot water
Their idea of difficult cooking.
THIS IS WHERE IT GETS ROUGH, ISN'T IT?

ピー
SQUEAK
OOH ...
WE'VE GOT ALL THAT DONE.

THREE LEFT, YEAH.
Onigiri
Fried chicken
Tamagoyaki
Cabbage
THREE LEFT?

I JUST NEED TO MAKE SOMETHING OMELETTE-ISH RIGHT?
HUH?

Huh?
OH, BUT...
...I CAN MAKE TAMAGO-YAKI.
SENSEI! YOU'RE AMAZ-ING!
I think...

TAMAGOYAKI IS WHEN YOU PILE A BUNCH OF THIN, THIN LAYERS OF EGG ON TOP OF EACH OTHER!
IT'S SWEET!
I KNOW!
SENSEI, THAT'S NOT...
CLATTER

Y-YOU'RE ABSOLUTELY RIGHT.
PAT
PAT

THAT'S WHAT TAMAGO-YAKI IS, RIGHT?

...
LOOKS LIKE YOU'RE NOT GETTING OUT OF IT, SENSEI. HEH HEH.
Heh heh...

...
I WANT TO...
Huh?
MAYBE HE'S STILL UPSET ABOUT BURNING THE EGGS THE OTHER DAY.
Sigh...
I WASN'T TRYING TO GET OUT OF IT.
I THOUGHT IT WOULD BE BETTER THAN FAILING.

...MAKE A DELICIOUS LUNCH...
...THAT WILL GET TSUMUGI ALL EXCITED.

I WANT TO MAKE HER HAPPY...
...JUST LIKE YOU WANT TO MAKE YOUR MOM HAPPY.

I THINK THAT...
...HAVING SEEN HOW HARD YOU WORKED TO MAKE IT...
Ha ha
Heh...
AT LEAST, I WOULD BE IF I WERE HER.
I, UH...
THANK YOU...
I DON'T KNOW ...
...BUT IF I HAD A DAD, MAYBE THIS IS WHAT HE'D BE LIKE.
OKAY.
...SHE WON'T CARE IF IT'S GOOD OR NOT.
SHE'LL BE HAPPY.

OKAY, BETTER GET READY FOR THIS, TSUMUGI!
THREE EGGS.
A TEA-SPOON OF SUGAR.
SALT... IN YOU GO!
CRACK
CLENCH

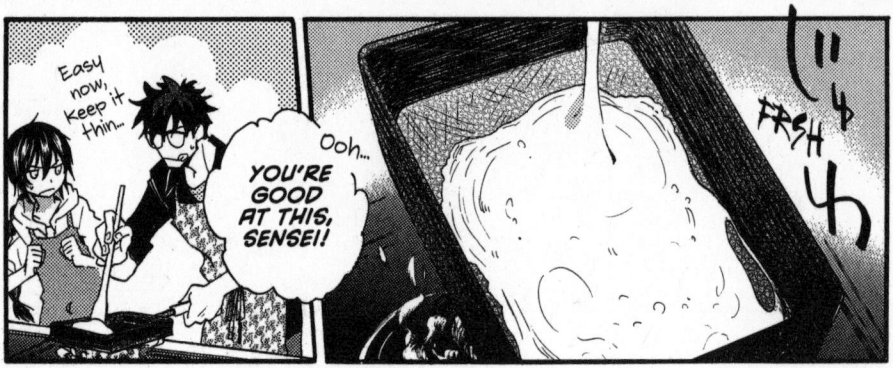
Easy now, keep it thin...
Ooh...
YOU'RE GOOD AT THIS, SENSEI!
FRSH

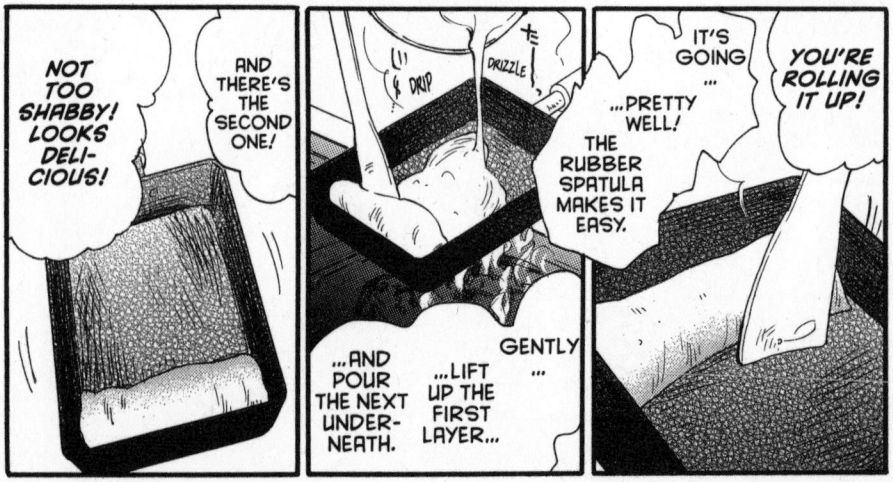
NOT TOO SHABBY! LOOKS DELI-CIOUS!
AND THERE'S THE SECOND ONE!
DRIP
DRIZZLE
...AND POUR THE NEXT UNDER-NEATH.
...LIFT UP THE FIRST LAYER...
GENTLY ...
IT'S GOING ...
...PRETTY WELL!
THE RUBBER SPATULA MAKES IT EASY.
YOU'RE ROLLING IT UP!

ALL RIGHT, NOW FOR THE THIRD ONE...
SPLAT
AAAAH!
AAAH!
I PUT IN TOO MUCH!
AAAH
PLOP
WHAT DO WE DO? WHAT'S GOING TO HAPPEN WITH THIS THING?
UH... LET'S JUST MAKE AN OMELETTE!
MIX IT ALL UP, STIR IT TOGETHER!
THEN HEAT IT THROUGH!
HUH?
LET'S TRY CUTTING IT OPEN, OKAY?
SENSEI ...

Ooh!
NICE!
IT LOOKS DELICIOUS!
RIGHT, TSUMUGI-CHAN?
THIS IS IT!
THIS IS THE ONE I SAW ON TV!
IT DOESN'T LOOK RIGHT.
S...
SORRY.
FLUFF
ふわっ
Wah!
OKAY!
THE FRIED CHICKEN! I'LL TRY HARD ON THE FRIED CHICKEN NEXT!
...HAVE TO GET SO DOWN.
...
SQUEEZE
Sakura-Shrimp and Corn Onigiri
YOU DON'T ...
Um...
YOU ADD WATER, RIGHT?
SLOSH
THAT'S WHAT MY MOM SAID!
YES! ADDING MOISTURE MAKES FOR PLUMP, JUICY FRIED CHICKEN.
OKAY!
ドキ ドキ
BA-DUM
BA-DUM
I'M GONNA DO IT...
SIZZLE
じゅわ...
I'M GONNA FRY IT!
THIS IS MY CHANCE TO ATONE FOR THE TAMAGO-YAKI!

SENSEI, KEEP PUTTING THEM IN!
Waah!
OKAY!
JERK
SIZZLE-POP
OW, HOT!!
EEGH!
It splashed me!
WAAAAAH!
TWO-STEP FRYING, SENSEI!
LIKE THIS?! LIKE THIS, MAYBE?
TAKE THEM OUT AND THEN PUT THEM BACK IN! OUT, OUT!
GRAB
GRAB
LET THEM REST!
Waaaah!
SENSEI! PUT THEM IN!
THEN PUT THEM IN!
WHOOSH

CRUNCH
さく
CHOMP
CHEW...
OH.
TASTE TEST, PLEASE.
I WISH I'D DONE IT WITH HIM.
WHEW!
YUP!
YUP!
...WHILE THEY'RE STILL WARM.
はったー STEP
はったー STEP
Oh.
I'LL MIX THEM ...
...WITH THE SWEET 'N' SPICY SAUCE...
I'M SO GLAD...
WAS THE FRIED CHICKEN A SUCCESS?
YUP! JUST YOU WAIT!

THE FRIED CHICKEN GOES HERE.
IT'S A FRIED CHICKEN FARM!
HEAVEN'S UP ABOVE, SO THAT'S WHERE YOU PUT THE EGGS!
SAME WITH THE CHIKUWA!
'CAUSE IT'S WHITE?
YUP!
THERE'S ONE LEFT OVER.
ぱく
CHOMP
!!
SNEAKING A BITE IS THE BEST PART OF PACKING LUNCH!
I'M GONNA DO IT, TOO!
IS THAT OKAY?!
ARE YOU ALLOWED TO DO THAT?
CHEW
もぐ
Heh heh.

Ah!
MAKE SURE YOU LEAVE ENOUGH TO EAT LATER!
Just a bite, just a bite...
RING RING
OH.
HI, MOM!
YEAH, I JUST GOT DONE MAKING IT.

YEAH.
YEAH.
I SEE.

IT'S FINE. YOU CAN'T HELP IT.
ARE YOU GONNA BE OKAY?
ARE YOU GETTING ENOUGH SLEEP? ARE YOU SURE YOU'RE NOT WORKING TOO MUCH?
I DON'T WANT YOU COLLAPSING, OKAY?

CAN YOU DO ME A FAVOR?
SO, SENSEI.
YUP. SHE SKIPPED OUT ON ME AGAIN!
UM... WAS THAT...?
...YEAH.
BYE.

SNAP

I'LL EAT THIS WITH MY MOM WHEN SHE COMES BACK TONIGHT.
I'M FINE.
NO, IT'S FINE.
IT'S FINE, BUT...
...ARE YOU OKAY?
THANKS! I'LL SEND THIS TO MY MOM!

RUSTLE
RUSTLE
RUMBLE
LET'S INVITE KOTORI-CHAN...
TSU-MUGI.
WE SAID WE'D ONLY PLAY WITH HER AT HER RESTAU-RANT, RIGHT?
VRRROOM
...
HEY...

!
PLIP
POURRRRR
PLIP
PLIP
...
...SAID IT'D BE CLEAR.
WAH ?!
NO WAY! THE WEATHER REPORT...
TSU-MUGI...
I'M SORRY, TSUMUGI.

WOW!
WHAT THE HECK?
RISE
IT'S DELI-CIOUS!

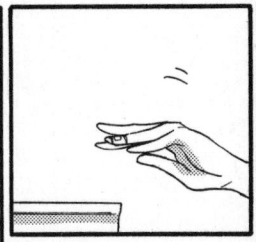

CHEW

...

I'll ask her about it.
HUH? THE CABBAGE AND SHIRASU TASTES REALLY... BLAND.
I THINK MOM'S IS BETTER.
I MADE THE RICE FIRMER TODAY, AND IT'S REALLY GOOD.
WOW! IT'S SO GOOD!
THE TAMAGO-YAKI TURNED OUT JUST FINE!
I'M GLAD THE MARINADE DIDN'T GET TOO SALTY.

WHAT A GREAT GOLDEN WEEK.

WE MADE ALL THIS...
...BY OUR-SELVES.

CLATTER
Huh?
SEN-SEI?!
WHAT HAPP...
Oh, wow...
RAIN?!
POUR
THAT'S RIGHT. IT'S RAINING.
SO...
...CAN WE...
...EAT HERE?

YES.
ばっ
POP
ふっ
W...
WOW!
Wow!
A TENT!
IT'S JUST A NAPTIME TOY.
I'm glad I brought it.
Sorry to put it up on your tatami mats...
No, it's perfectly fine.

I WANNA EAT OUR LUNCHES, DADDY!
OH, YEAH.
IT'S LUNCH-TIME ALREADY.
HEE HEE HEE HEE!
COME IN, DADDY!
HUH?!
RUSTLE
RUSTLE
OKAY, JUST YOU WAIT!
ISN'T IT A LITTLE TOO TINY?
I JUST BARELY FIT... YOU OKAY, TSUMUGI?
THIS IS SO MUCH FUN!!
I...
I ALREADY ATE MY SHARE.
IT'S OKAY. YOU CAN HAVE SOME OF MINE. SHOULDN'T GO TO WASTE.

WOW ...!

YUM...
Tsumugi, the veggies are yummy too!
Ptoo! I'm not eating celery!
MAYBE SHE JUST...
...DOESN'T WANT TO EAT THE SAME THING AGAIN.
THE SAUCE?!
WHAT'S THIS SWEET 'N' SPICY STUFF WITH THE SESAME SEEDS?
IT'S GOOD!
NOM
The marinade really-soaked-in!
BUT THE ONES WITHOUT THE SWEET AND SPICY SAUCE ARE ALSO GOOD!
NOM
THE FRIED CHICKEN IS SO YUMMY!
Fried chicken!
FRIED CHICK-EN!!
FRIED CHICK-EN!!
Bouncy, bouncy!!
YOU REALLY DO LOVE MEAT, DON'T YOU, TSUMUGI?
Juicy!!
I CAN'T EAT ANY MORE.
You eat the celery, Daddy!
Celery!
Eat the celery!
I FEEL ...
... SO FULL...

Sweet and Spicy

FRIED CHICKEN

☆ Ingredients ☆ Serves 3-4

300 g chicken (thighs)
a little potato starch
cold water
1/2 Tbsp white sesame seeds

Ⓐ 3 Tbsp soy sauce 2 Tbsp sake
1 tsp grated ginger 1 tsp minced garlic

Ⓑ 2 Tbsp soy sauce 1 Tbsp sugar 1 Tbsp mirin

1. Cut **chicken** into bite-sized chunks and soak in **cold water** for 10 minutes.
2. Take the **chicken** out of the water and gently pat dry. Mix the ingredients listed in **A** and marinate **chicken** for 10 minutes.
3. Lightly coat the **chicken** with **potato starch** and fry at 160° C for a minute and a half. When the surface turns light brown, take the pieces out and let them rest for 3 minutes. Increase the oil temperature to 190° C and fry again for 40 seconds.

4. Put all the ingredients listed in **B** into a saucepan and mix. Place the pan on medium heat. Once it boils down, add the **white sesame seeds.**
5. Pour **4** evenly over **3**.

CONVERSION NOTES:
300 G CHICKEN = ABOUT 10 1/2 OZ, 160° C = 320° F, 190° C = 375° F

Nagoya Chicken Wing
Sweet 'n Spicy Sauce
I think that's it...
I wish I could remember it!
Yum yum
What is it?
I know this taste...
Hmm... I've had this sauce somewhere before.
?

TSUMUGI-CHAN'S BARELY EATING HER LUNCH!
SENSEI!
HUH?
HOLD ON A SECOND.
OH MY.
STEP
STEP
WHAT'S WRONG? ARE YOU FULL?
LET'S TAKE YOUR TEMPERA-TURE!
FLUSH

DAZE
IF YOU'RE THAT INTERESTED IN HER, ASK HER TO JOIN US!
YEAH, ASK HER YOURSELF.
IIDA-SAN'S FROZEN STILL.
Oh, look.
CLATTER
B-BUT SHE'S ALWAYS EATING SOMETHING DURING BREAKS.
SHE DOESN'T SEEM TO BE EMBARRASSED ABOUT EATING ALONE. MAYBE THAT'S JUST HER POLICY OR SOMETHING...

KOTORI!
YOU MAKE ANY FRIENDS YET?
HUH?
NOT YET!
YOU'RE SO SLOW! EVEN IF YOU'RE FINE WITH BEING ALONE, YOU SHOULD AT LEAST MAKE A FEW!
Ha ha ha!
YOUR CLASS IS NEXT DOOR.
WHAT ARE YOU DOING HERE?
Friends from middle school
I CAME TO SEE HOW YOU WERE DOING!
SORRY I COULDN'T HANG OUT OVER GOLDEN WEEK.
Aaah
I ENDED UP HAVING TO SPEND THE WHOLE TIME TAKING CARE OF MY LITTLE BROTHERS.
WHAT DID YOU DO OVER GOLDEN WEEK, KOTORI?

You ate octopus?
What? Octopus?
GOLDEN WEEK...
... SURE WAS FUN.
S...
SEN-SE-
ガラッ
CLATTER
Ssh!
YES.
I SEE.
YES.

SO HOW'S SHE DOING?
A FEVER. I SEE.
NO COUGH.
I SEE.
OH.
IT'S FINE. I'LL BE RIGHT THERE.
YES.
THANK YOU VERY MUCH.

SEN-SEI?
OH, TSU-MUGI IS...
THAT IS, MY KID ISN'T FEELING WELL...
Ah!
SORRY. I'LL BE GOING HOME EARLY.

...

HEFT
Feel better soon!
Take care!
SHE'S HOT...
IT'S BEEN A YEAR SINCE THE LAST TIME SHE GOT SICK.
WHY DIDN'T I...
...NOTICE THIS MORNING?
RECEPTION
IS THAT WHY?
AH!
GOLDEN WEEK

THAT'S WHAT YOU DO, RIGHT?
うろうろ PACE
CHANGE HER PJS.
LET HER SWEAT A LOT.
MAKE SURE SHE'S WARM.
PLENTY OF WATER.
うろうろ PACE
Wheeze
TSUMUGI GOT SICK, AND...
YEAH, IT'S KÔHEI.
OH, MOM?
RING RING
ガチャ CLICK
...
YES, THANK YOU!
I SHOULD MAKE SURE SHE'S WARM, AND SWEATS A LOT, AND GETS PLENTY OF WATER, RIGHT?
YEAH!
I WENT TO THE DOCTOR ALREADY!

YEAH, YOU TOO.
BYE.
CLICK
DOOOOOT
IT'S FINE. YOU'VE GOT GRANNIE TO TAKE CARE OF.
ARE HER KNEES OKAY? MAKE SURE SHE USES HER CANE.
YES.
YOU, TOO.
Ha ha.

TSUMUGI.
PAT トン トン PAT

Sigh...

SHAKE ふる
SHAKE ふる

YOU COULDN'T EAT YOUR LUNCH, RIGHT? ARE YOU HUNGRY?
HOW IS YOUR STOMACH FEELING?

THE SPECIAL...
OKAY. IF THERE'S ANYTHING YOU WANT TO EAT, LET ME KNOW.
...
OKAY. I'LL BUY IT... ...WHEN I GO GET DIN-NER.
I was in such a hurry.
RIGHT... I SHOULD'VE BOUGHT IT.
HUH? OH! OH! RIGHT, RIGHT! THE SPECIAL!
DING DONG!
ピンポーン
UGH...
Huff
Wheeze
ARE YOU GOING SOME-WHERE?

WHO COULD THAT BE...?
ガチャ
CLICK
I...
I CAME IN DISGUISE...
TOSS!
ぽいっ
YOU LOOK REALLY SUSPICIOUS!!
D-DO I?
バシン
SLAM
WHAT'S GOTTEN INTO YOU?

I...
I WAS WORRIED!
ABOUT TSUMUGI-CHAN!
AND YOU WERE IN SUCH A HURRY.
SO I CAME TO CHECK IN ON YOU.
I BROUGHT ONIONS AND GINGER AND A LOT OF OTHER THINGS I THOUGHT SHE COULD EAT...
...
I...
I'M SORRY.
NOW THAT I'VE CALMED DOWN...
...I REALIZE IT'S REALLY WEIRD TO JUST SHOW UP LIKE THIS.
YOU'RE FREAKED OUT, AREN'T YOU?
OH!
OH, RIGHT!
QUICK! I'LL BE RIGHT BACK...
...SO CAN YOU STAY AND WATCH THE HOUSE FOR A MINUTE?
HUH?

They moved to the living room.

I WON'T GIVE UP!
AS LONG AS I HAVE THESE STRONG FEELINGS AND A HEART THAT BELIEVES...
...MY WISH WILL COME TRUE!
THAT'S MOMMY.
どさっ
BA-DUMP

I HEARD THAT WHEN I'M AN OLD LADY, I'LL BE ABLE TO SEE HER AGAIN.
SO I DON'T FEEL LONELY.
AND ALSO, I THINK I'LL BE ABLE TO SEE HER SOONER.
Some-how.
...
I SEE.
...
UM...
WOULD YOU LET ME BE YOUR FRIEND?

I see!
WE WERE ALREADY FRIENDS!
KEH KEH!
THAT'S RIGHT!
I THOUGHT MAYBE IT WOULD MAKE YOU FEEL A LITTLE LESS LONELY...
?
I THOUGHT YOU WERE ALREADY MY FRIEND.
Huh?
Huff
Huff
I BOUGHT IT!
Welcome back!
Oh!
DADDY'S BACK!
I'M BACK!
CAN: WHITE PEACHES
白桃

THE "YOU GOT A COLD" SPECIAL...
Mmph
AAAH
じゅわ
SLURP
はっ
JUMP
Yay!
ZZZ...
She ate it all.
I'M ALL BETTER NOW...
STAGGER
ふらっ
Oh...
GO BACK TO BED.
ふらっ
STAGGER
Heh heh.
WHEN I GOT COLDS, I USED TO EAT CANNED PEACHES, TOO.
I SEE.
FOR ME, IT WAS ALWAYS APPLE SAUCE.

Hmm...
I HAD RICE PORRIDGE AND SOFT UDON NOODLES.
BUT WHAT'S BREAD POR-RIDGE?
YOU TEAR UP SOME BREAD AND SIMMER IT IN MILK 'TIL IT GETS SOUPY.
IT'S NICE TO HAVE A SPECIAL MEAL YOU ONLY EAT WHEN YOU'RE SICK.
Ah
AND THERE WAS VEGGIE SOUP AND BREAD POR-RIDGE...
COLD CHAWAN-MUSHI...
Oh.
NOT AT ALL. THANKS FOR YOUR HELP.
...I'M SORRY I'VE STAYED SO LONG...
OH!
You add in sugar or honey to make it sweet.
Ahh... it's so delicious.
UH...
UM...
...

Whew
THAT WOULD BE SUCH A HUGE HELP!
IF YOU'RE GOING TO MAKE SOMETHING, DO YOU WANT ME TO HELP?
Oh!
RIGHT!
WE NEED TO ASK HER FIRST.
I THINK WE CAN MAKE THAT.
LET'S ASK TSUMUGI-CHAN IF THERE'S ANYTHING SHE WANTS TO EAT.
I'M SO GLAD!
OKAY, WHAT SHOULD WE MAKE?
Hmm...
I'M INTERESTED IN THIS BREAD PORRIDGE STUFF. RICE PORRIDGE IS EASY. OR WE COULD ALSO DO UDON...OR CHAWANMUSHI LIKE YOU MENTIONED.
What ingredients do you have on hand?
Um, this and this and this...
Hmm?

A DELIVERY MENU!
Ooh!
Ta-da!
IT'S A MENU!
Menu
· Rice Porridge
· Nyuumen
· Udon
· Bread Porridge
· Veggie Soup
TODAY WE'RE HAVING DELIVERY FROM DADDY'S RESTAURANT.

WHAT?
Oh.
YOU'RE UP.
ARE YOU GUYS DOING SOMETHING?
MRK

NEW men.
Oh, I see.
WE'RE GONNA EAT IT TOGETHER, RIGHT?
CAN YOU EAT ALL THAT?
Oh...
AND THIS!
THIS AND THIS!
TAP
TAP
TAP
Menu
Porridge
Nyuumen
Udon
Egg
WHICH DO YOU WANT TO EAT?
HMMMM...

We'll make all the dashi stock at once...
...and make the chawan-mushi first.
HMM...
HMM... SOUNDS DELICIOUS!
NYUUMEN AND CHAWAN-MUSHI.
And apples.
WHAT DO YOU THINK OF THIS ORDER?

PACKAGES: KONBU (TOP), KATSUO (BOTTOM)

BOX: INSTANT DASHI

ONCE IT STARTS TO SINK, YOU TURN OFF THE HEAT.
CLICK カチ

Then add lots of katsuo-bushi.
BUBBLE ふつふつ

THEN YOU WAIT FOR IT TO SINK ALL THE WAY...
...TO THE BOT-TOM.

BUT WHEN I WAS A KID, I USED TO LOVE WATCHING MY MOM MAKE IT.
IT WAS ALWAYS SO EXCITING!
MAYBE THAT'S WHY I'M EXCITED NOW.

THIS IS ACTUALLY THE FIRST TIME I'M MAKING MY OWN STOCK.
Heh!

YOU LOOK REALLY EXCITED.
HUH?

GENTLY STRAIN IT...
...AND THEN...
IT CAME OUT REALLY NICE.

IT'S REALLY PURE.
IT'S LIKE...
IT... IT'S GOOD...
REALLY ?
!
THE FIRST THING WE'LL USE THIS DASHI FOR IS THE CHAWANMUSHI!
Oh! I GUESS I REALLY CAN'T TELL. I'M SORRY.
I've never understood the difference between the store-bought ones, either.
Ugh.
But it feels like it would be good for you.
Beat the eggs.
Pour the dashi, soy sauce, sake, and salt through a strainer when you add it.
Mix it carefully so you don't get bubbles...
I...I'll cut up the mitsuba.
Okay.

THIS IS EXCITING!
Heh heh!
Now, before you pour the liquid in...
...AND CHECK OUT THIS KAMABOKO!
OOH!
SLICED MAGI-GAL KAMABOKO
STRAIN THE EGG MIXTURE...
Put either aluminum foil or a cloth napkin on top.
Like this.
DON'T WORRY. YOU CAN USE A POT.
Fill the water to a third of the way up the chawan cups.
...give it two minutes on high, then 15-20ish on low.
AH...
Once it starts boiling...
(Yes, he does)
YOU DON'T HAVE A STEAMER, DO YOU?
HMM... PROBABLY NOT?
THAT'S FINE.
SORRY, I'M LEAVING THAT TO YOU.
I SHOULD CUT THE VEGGIES FIRST, RIGHT?
...WHILE IT'S STEAMING.
LET'S GET THE NYUU-MEN READY...

I'VE BEEN...
...STARTING TO REALLY LIKE IT.
トン
CHOP
SO LEAVE IT TO ME.
CHOP
トン
CHOP
トン
CHOP
トン
RIGHT!

OOH... IT LOOKS DELICIOUS ALREADY...
But let's add mirin and soy sauce.
WHEN SHOULD WE COOK THE SOMEN NOODLES?
OH, I WANT TO COOL THE CHAWAN-MUSHI FIRST.

PUT THE...
...HARDER VEGETABLES INTO THE STOCK FIRST.
BUBBLE
くつ
BUBBLE
くつ

MOMMY ...
IT TAKES TIME, BUT YOU REALLY CAN MAKE YOUR OWN STOCK, HUH?
TOSS
SO-MEN NOODLES
Well...
IT'S A PAIN TO DO. I THINK YOU'RE FINE USING THE STORE-BOUGHT STUFF.
Then why did we...?
HUH?
BUT ...
...IT DOESN'T HURT TO KNOW HOW TO MAKE IT.

FOR SOME REASON ...
...I REALLY WANTED YOU TO GO FOR IT TODAY...
...TO BE EVEN NICER THAN USUAL...
...TO TSUMUGI-CHAN.

THAT SMELLS GOOD.
RUB むぎゅー
WHAT IS IT?

Huh?
YOU'RE THE ONE WHO DID ALL THE WORK TODAY.
NO, IT WAS YOU!
HEY!

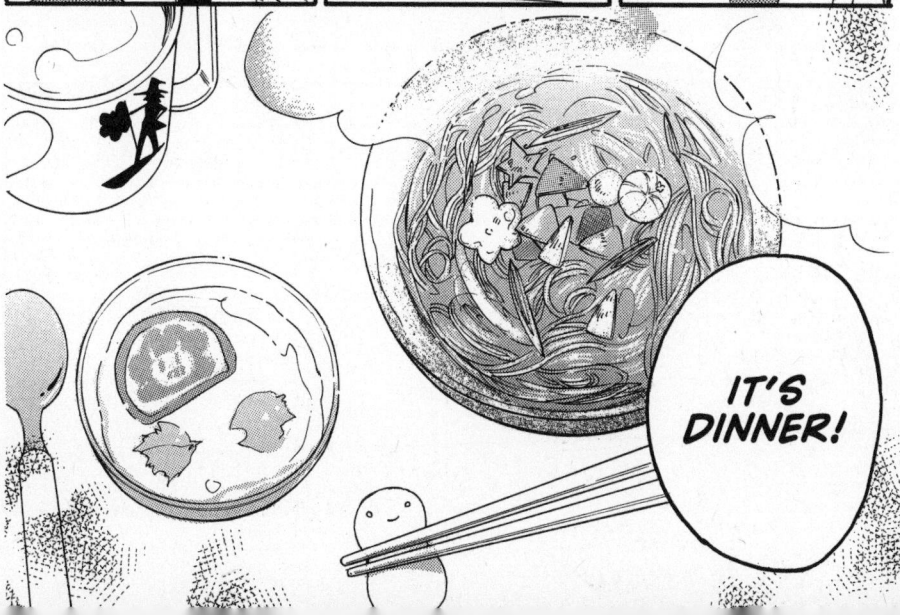
IT'S DINNER!

ちゅるん
SLURP
MMM...
MR. GALI GALI'S KAMABOKO?!
Her temperature's going up.
Huh?
OOH!
HERE, THERE'S HOT NYUU-MEN, TOO.
I'M GLAD YOU'RE FEELING BETTER.
YOU'RE RIGHT.
YUM!
SO SILKY SMOOTH! ♡
IT'S SO GOOD!
FFFH
FFFH
UH...
FINE...
HUH?
BLOW ON IT, DADDY!
ニヤリ
ニヤリ

GOBBLE はっ
GOBBLE はっ
IT'S SO GOOD...

Ooh!
THERE WAS A TIME WHEN YOU WERE IN HIGH SCHOOL?
OF COURSE THERE WAS.
I guess I'm an older guy now.
SLIDE すり
しゃり SLICE
I USED TO EAT THIS FOR A LATE-NIGHT SNACK IN HIGH SCHOOL ALL THE TIME.
Salt water
THIS BRINGS BACK SO MANY MEMO-RIES.

I...
I'M GOING HOME!
HUH?
But the apples are still...
CLICK ガチャ
TSUMUGI-CHAN, FEEL BETTER!
IF...

THANKS SO MUCH.
Ha ha!
THE APPLES! ADD A LITTLE OF THAT ORANGE JUICE IN THE FRIDGE AND THEY'LL LOOK GOOD AND TASTE GOOD!
Oh!
ARE YOU OKAY?
TAKE CARE...

Chapter 5 - END

CHAWANMUSHI

Maybe we'll use home-made next time.

For the pork miso soup, we used store-bought stock.

Dashi Stock

☆ Ingredients ☆ Serves 3-4

1 L water
40 g katsuobushi
10 cm sq piece konbu

Steps

1. Put the **water** and **konbu** into a stockpot on medium heat, and take out the **konbu** just before it boils.
2. Add the **katsuobushi** to the pot. Once the **katsuobushi** starts to sink, turn off the heat and remove scum from the stock's surface. Once the katsuobushi completely sinks, strain it gently.

POINT If you squeeze the **katsuobushi** while straining, the dashi won't taste right, so be careful!

Tastes great hot or chilled!

Chawanmushi

☆ Ingredients ☆ Serves 3-4

3 eggs kamaboko, mitsuba to taste

Ⓐ 450 cc dashi stock (3x the amount of eggs)
1 tsp soy sauce 1 tsp sake
1 scant tsp salt

POINT You can add whatever else you want: shrimp, chicken, shiitake mushrooms, lily bulbs, gingko nuts, etc.

Steps

1. Beat the **eggs**, making sure that bubbles don't form. Add the ingredients from **A**. Mix carefully and then strain!
2. Cut the **kamaboko** into bite-sized pieces. Place a couple in the bottom of each dish before pouring in the egg mix from **step 1**. Cover each cup with aluminum foil.
3. Fill a big pot with water, about one third of the height of the cups, and heat. When the water boils, put the cups from **step 2** into the pot. Put the lid on the pot loosely, and after 2 minutes turn to low heat.
4. After the cups steam for 15-20 minutes, remove and place **mitsuba** on the egg surface. Reseal with aluminum foil and let steam a little longer.

CONVERSION NOTES:
1 L WATER = ABOUT 4 1/4 CUPS, 40 G KATSUOBUSHI = ABOUT 1.5 OZ, 10 CM KONBU = 4 IN., 450 CC DASHI = 2 CUPS

Plain chawanmushi is still good.
Lotte's late night snack

SIGNS: A REAL OPTOMETRIST (TOP), WE HAVE CONTACTS (BOTTOM)

BUN: MEAT

※KOTORI WORE A BLAZER IN HIGH SCHOOL, BUT HERE SHE'S SHOWN WEARING A SAILOR UNIFORM, DUE TO AUTHORIAL PREFERENCE.

YOU CAN DO IT, KOTORI...!
OKAY.
FIRST WE'LL EXAMINE YOUR EYES TO SEE IF YOU'RE OKAY TO WEAR CONTACT LENSES.
I'M SUPPOSED TO PUT THESE IN MY EYES?!
THEY'RE PRETTY BIG...
STUNNED
Here...
LET'S TRY PUTTING THEM IN.
HMM... YOU'RE JUST FINE.
huff
huff
OKAY!
Hyah...
HYAAAHH!

SIGNS: YUMMY RAMEN (TOP), CHINESE (BOTTOM)

STEAM
モファー
ズバーン
TA-DA!
SCARF
はっふー
ずばばばっ
SLURP
SLURP
SLURP
ずばばばっ
SLURP
SLURP
SLURP
MAYBE I'LL TRY THOSE CONTACTS, AFTER ALL.
Oh?
BLURRY
ギャー
RUB
こし
RUB
こし

The End

Afterword

See you next volume!

雨隠 ギド
Gido Amagakure

Thank you!

Koz, Gon-chan, Tsuru-san, W-yama-san
O-hara-san, M-chan, E-san, Nori-chan

T-shiro-sama, Jun Abe-sama
Research Support: Tabegoto-ya Norabo-sama
Cooking Advisor: Yo Tatewaki-sama

Thank you for all for your help!!

Translation Notes

Flower viewing, page 10: Flower viewing refers to Hanami, the Japanese tradition of viewing flowers in full bloom. Though this may include any type of flower, it mostly refers to cherry blossoms and, less often, plum blossoms. Hanami is typically done in spring and is often enjoyed as a picnic-like activity where friends, family, and coworkers eat prepared meals while observing the beauty of flowers in bloom.

Donabe, page 26: A special type of clay pot used for cooking over an open flame.

Nozawana, miso beef, and iwanori seaweed, page 39: Nozawana is a type of Japanese mustard leaf that if often pickled. Miso beef or *nikumiso* is a mixture of ground beef and miso. Iwanori (rock seaweed) is a type of seaweed found between rocks that is typically dried for consumption. All three of these foods are typically used as condiments or rice toppings.

The role of a teacher, page 54: In Japan, the role of a teacher can sometimes be a little different from that of their Western counterparts. Japanese teachers may be more directly involved in the life of students inside and outside school, almost functioning as second parents. Though there is a clearer line between teacher and student these days, in the past, the student-teacher relationship was much more intimate, and it wasn't uncommon for teachers to spend time with their students and their students' families outside of school.

Thumbprint, page 56: Though signing one's name has become fairly common in Japan, ink stamps/seals and thumbprints are still used to sign documents.

Salisbury steak, page 58: In Japan, this dish is called *hanbaagu* or may also be called hamburg steak. *Hanbaagu* is a standard of *goshoku* (Western-style cooking) and you'll find some version of it in almost every *famiresu* (family-style restaurant) in Japan.

Konnyaku, page 59: A starchy plant also known as "devil's tongue." It's made into a gelatin form and used as an ingredient in Japanese dishes.

Golden Week, page 113: In early May, a series of holidays form a week of vacation, allowing many students and families to travel or spend time together.

Shirasu, page 117: Dried baby anchovies.

Chikuwa, page 117: A tube-shaped food product made from fish paste, starch, and other ingredients.

Konbu, page 122: A type of thick kelp that is often dried and used in the preparation of soup stock.

Tatami mats, page 140: A type of traditional Japanese flooring tupically made of rice straw.

Chawanmushi, page 164: A savory, steamed egg custard eaten as a main dish in Japan. Chawanmushi directly translates to "steamed (in) tea bowl" and the dish itself is traditionally served in a tea bowl.

Nyuumen, page 166: Thin wheat-flour noodles in a broth with vegetables, meat, and any number of other ingredients.

Katsuobushi, page 167: Dried, fermented skipjack tuna that is typically shaved off into flakes. It is also used to prepare soup stock.

Kamaboko, page 171: A type of processed fish paste primarily made from pureed whitefish and formed into a loaf that can be sliced i.

Tsumugi doesn't want to eat her green peppers.

The dinner table freezes.